Enneagram Self Discovery

A Self Awareness and Personal Growth Journey to Understanding Yourself and Find Your Personality Type

I0414761

Written By

Beto Canales & Habits of Wisdom

purposes only. All effort has been executed to present accurate, up to date, and reliable, complete information. No warranties of any kind are declared or implied. Readers acknowledge that the author is not engaging in the rendering of legal, financial, medical or professional advice. The content within this book has been derived from various sources. Please consult a licensed professional before attempting any techniques outlined in this book.

By reading this document, the reader agrees that under no circumstances is the author responsible for any losses, direct or indirect, which are incurred as a result of the use of information contained within this document, including, but not limited to, — errors, omissions, or inaccuracies.

Table of Contents

Introduction

You probably have not put a lot of thought into your personality, and its type, however, it is highly important for everyone to know their personality types. That is because if they knew their personality types and everything that there is to know about themselves, it would greatly influence them on going into areas of their lives that best suits them.

With that said, if people understood their personality types, they would only go into careers that best suits them. Additionally, this would also influence them on whether or not they should settle down, get married, or even have kids. Or, if they do choose to get married based on their personality type, they would be pickier as far as who to hook up with based on knowing whether he or she would be the right fit. This would lead to fewer divorces and many more happy marriages as opposed to being married out of convenience.

In other words, if people knew more about their personality types, then they would be happier in general, they would be at peace, and simply be more comfortable in their own skin. They could also become the best versions of themselves which would bring them the ultimate happiness. And that means they would be able to once and for all banish confusion, and the good news is that they can! You are now wondering how can people possibly know what personality type they have?

They would do that by becoming familiar with the Enneagram which is a tool that is extremely powerful when it comes to learning about who you are and using it to transform you in incredible ways!

Before going into the nitty gritty of the Enneagram, you will need to know about the history of it in order to understand its origin and purpose. This will be discussed in the first chapter.

Chapter 1: The History Of The Enneagram

This may be the first time you have ever heard of the term Enneagram, or if not, you likely don't know much about it. And, in this chapter, the history of the Enneagram will be covered. The references are derived from the 1994 paperback *The Enneagram Made Easy: Discover the 9 Types of People* which was written by the late author, Elizabeth Wagele, and therapist Renee Baron.

The history of the Enneagram is still quite unknown. However, the origin of the word Enneagram is derived from the Greek, *enna* which means nine, and *gramma* which means something that is drawn or written. With that said, the Enneagram is also referred to as the Enneagram Of Personality. What it is, presents the human psyche and the 9 personality types or they are referred to as the enneatypes.

The origin of this model comes from over a century ago, and it has influences from the late Russian mystic and philosopher, George Ivanovich Gurdjieff. However, it is unknown whether the emergence of the Enneagram came from the Chilean-born psychologist, Claudio Benjamín Naranjo Cohen, or the Bolivian-born psychologist, Óscar Ichazo. However, both of these psychologists from South America had used the Enneagram Of Personality in their teachings. And both psychologists were founders and pioneers of important aspects of psychology.

However, since it the Enneagram derived from the teachings of possibly both psychologists, you will want to know about the history of Óscar Ichazo and Claudio Benjamín Naranjo Cohen, and what their roles were. The history of Óscar Ichazo will be covered in the following section of this chapter.

The History Of Óscar Ichazo

Óscar Ichazo was born in July 1931 in Bolivia,

and he was the founder of the Arica School in 1968 which was named after Arica, Chile where he once lived. This school is a human potential movement group has anyone who had studied at this institute will have learned methods on how to raise cosmic consciousness. And, according to his that was written in 1982, *Interviews With Oscar Ichazo*, he became interested in psychology in 1954 as he started to study the behavior and thought pattern repeating itself. And then he discovered along the way there are 9 ways that an individual's ego will settle within the psyche during the first years of childhood.

And the more he studied this phenomenon, he had found connections between the 9 different personalities and mapped out the circle, the lines, and the points. This is how the Enneagram came to be which he had used in his teachings when he had founded the Arica School in 1968. However, again, it is unknown if Ichazo had established the Enneagram, or if it was Claudio Benjamín Naranjo Cohen who had. In the final section of this chapter, more about Claudio Benjamín Naranjo Cohen will be covered.

The History of Claudio Benjamín Naranjo Cohen

Claudio Benjamín Naranjo Cohen or Claudio Naranjo was born in November 1932 and was a Chilean-born psychologist. He was considered the first to combine both spiritual as well as psychology into one, and he also founded the Seekers After Truth Institute, and he may have been the one to establish the Enneagram. His take on psychology was unique as he had incorporated spirituality with psychotherapy, and his way of teaching psychology and therapy methods were unique. In fact, the German-born psychologist Fritz Perls who founded Gestalt Therapy had named Claudio Naranjo as one of his 3 successors.

And, after years and years of studying psychology and spirituality, he had believed to have established the Enneagram which he had mentioned in his book from 1991, *Character and Neurosis: An Integrative View*. He had been extremely active in his studies and in his practice while he traveled all over the world to teach his findings and teach the principles of the Enneagram which is how he had become a renowned psychologist.

With that said, it is possible that both Claudio Naranjo and Oscar Ichazo had established the Enneagram because they are psychologists that have a unique way of studying the psyche. However, the likely reason that Ichazo was not said to be the one who had established this model is that some newer Enneagram of Personality writers had stated that he had published factual ideas which could not be copyrighted because of the fact that they were factual, he did not establish those theories.

Either way, regardless of which psychologist had established the Enneagram indicated that both have had a unique way of studying and analyzing the psyche because the Enneagram is essential for people to understand what they can about themselves.

As it was previously mentioned, the Enneagram model is there to help people in their business, personal, and in any aspect of their lives in general so that they receive a better understanding of themselves. And, before the age of Claudio Naranjo and Oscar Ichazo's work, this phenomenon was not considered because it was not known until both of these psychologists had started using its principles and using it in their teachings.

And, once the Enneagram is understood, and utilized by people, it will help them direct themselves towards the line of work they are the most suitable for, as well as the personality type of friends that they can make and maintain. And, this will help them attract the most suitable mate that has the personality type that would be well suited for them.

The Enneagram would help people avoid

situations that could lead them to failure and heartache which would have been a result of their doing by getting into situations that would not fit their personality type. On the other hand, sometimes people do need to experience failure and heartache regardless of the situation in order to evolve and to grow.

With that said, in the next chapter, you will learn about the details about the Enneagram before each of the 9 personality types are covered. And the references for these details are derived from *The Enneagram Made Easy: Discover the 9 Types of People*, written by the late author, Elizabeth Wagele, and therapist Renee Baron; as well as from *Personality Types: Using the Enneagram for Self-Discovery* that was written by Don Richard Riso who was an American teacher of the Enneagram of Personality and had formed the Enneagram Institute in 1997.

Chapter 2: Why The Enneagram Is Relevant To Everyone

The Enneagram is the most powerful tool for people to understand who they are as the late Don Richard Riso had stated in his books, including his paperback, *Personality Types: Using the Enneagram for Self-Discovery*. It has already been covered that the Enneagram represents 9 different personalities and archetypes which is meant to help people understand who they are, and why they act, think, and feel in relation to others, the world, and most importantly- themselves.

And, you may be thinking that the Enneagram represents those silly personality quizzes that you are told to take online to find out what personality matches your type. However, even though there may be a slight element of truth to that, what the Enneagram represents more than your personality type is that it delves quite deep into your fears, your strong motivations, and defense mechanisms. And these factors are what make up your personality as it is found buried deep underneath the structure of each personality.

Studies at Iowa State University have shown that there are positive effects of Enneagram on the well-being in a psychological way. Additionally, other studies have revealed that once young adults are aware of the effects of the Enneagram, they have an easier time accepting themselves.

Let's use the analogy of the onion and compare it to how the Enneagram picks apart your personality. The outer layer of the onion is what represents your general personality, and it is smooth. It is just the surface, and not much can be seen beyond that. However, once you start peeling that onion, then you start to see underneath the surface as the layers of the onion are removed. You see that it is not nearly as smooth as you dig deeper, and the smell of the onion is strong, and it can make you cry. The

Enneagram does the same to your personality, the outer layer of it. Once it is picked apart and layers are removed, then the core motivations, the deep-rooted fears, and the reason behind the defense mechanisms are found.

With that said, people learning their own personality type without peeling the outer layer will not learn much from it. Just like the surface layer of the onion does not add much flavor to your cooking. However, once each layer is removed, then people will learn a lot about why they are the way they are - and they can learn about how they relate to others and the world, as well as themselves. It will be uncomfortable to learn what makes up any personality, but in the end, it is quite helpful and healing. Just like how it is rough cutting an onion and removing the layers. The smell is strong, and it makes you cry. But once the inner parts of the onion are added to the meal that you are cooking, it provides the meal with a fantastic flavor.

And, people who have learned to use the

Enneagram for their benefit, they have in many ways healed and become at peace within themselves. They find out why they behave the way they do; they find out why they have the particular tastes that they have, and why they are repelled by certain things. And that doesn't mean that they have to fight their urges to be repelled by certain stimuli unless they want to heal from a particular phobia. In fact, they shouldn't do that, as that would go against their nature.

And, in order to fully understand the structure of the Enneagram, you will learn about the 9 personalities, as well as its wings and the center. In the next sections of this chapter, a brief overview of the personalities, the wings, and its centers will be covered before getting into the nitty-gritty of each one. The first thing to be covered is a brief overview of the 9 personalities.

The Overview Of The Nine Personality Types

Here is the part you have been looking forward to

about the Enneagram, as you will learn about the personality types that are part of its structure. The 9 personality types are:

- **Type One - The Perfectionist** - This type is known to have the need to get it right all the time, wants to keep improving everything, and is the responsible type.

- **Type Two - The Helper** - This type is the one that wants to help everyone and wants to always be the one that is needed in every situation.

- **Type Three - The Performer** - This type is the one who always wants to achieve something great and has to be successful because that is what validates this type.

- **Type Four - The Romantic** - This type is the one that believes that love can be regained from any failed situation or relationship and had an idealistic mindset.

And this type is incredibly empathetic.

- **Type Five - The Investigator** - This type is always the type to observe, study, and keep to themselves.

- **Type Six - The Loyalist** - This type has a difficult time trusting others and wants to trust but struggles to do so on a constant basis.

- **Type Seven - The Enthusiast** - This type is always looking for fun and adventure and are always looking forward to something in the future.

- **Type Eight - The Challenger** - This type is the one that has to be in control and is always up for a challenge. They are quite strong-willed and will never accept defeat.

- **Type Nine - The Peacemaker** - This type is always looking for peace and harmony and do what they can to avoid conflict at all costs.

Those are the 9 personalities that make up the Enneagram structure. There is a good chance that you have spotted several of these personalities that fit you the best. With that said, you may be thinking that several of these descriptions fit you the best, and not just one. That is why the Enneagram structure comes with wings and the centers which will be briefly discussed in the last section of this chapter.

The Wings And The Centers Of The Enneagram Structure

The wings of the Enneagram as it is referenced in late Riso's book, *Personality Types: Using the Enneagram for Self-Discovery* are the 2 types that are adjacent to your main type in the model. In other words, you can think of them as close neighbors that influence you but are not strong enough to have a huge impact on your core.

In order to help you understand this better, think

about getting an ice cream sundae. The flavor of the sundae will be vanilla, which is your core. But you will want to add something else to make the sundae flavored even more by adding fudge, caramel, and some sprinkles. The fudge, caramel, and the sprinkles will influence the flavor, but the main flavor will always be vanilla. That is what the wings of the Enneagram represent. They influence your core but don't change it. The wings are there to help people understand more about their core type, as well as how they relate to others and the world around them. And you can say as well that the wings are there to help balance the core.

The wings can help you problem-solve and gain a better understanding of life in general. That is what helps people stay balanced, just like an airplane that needs its wings to keep their core balanced while it is in the air. And, in addition to the wings, the Enneagram model also consists of 3 centers which are the negative aspects of any personality. The 3 centers are:

- **The Instinctive Center** as 3 personality types fall into this area and this area represents rage and anger

- **The Feeling Center** as 3 personality types also fall into this center and this area represents shame

- **The Thinking Center** as 3 personality types falls into this area as well, and this center represents fear.

And the personalities of the types that fall into the center are impacted by its emotional nature. However, more about the wings and the centers will be discussed later on in this eBook. The first thing that will be covered in the chapters to come are the 9 personality types of the Enneagram. And, the first personality that will be covered in the following chapter is Type One - The Perfectionist.

Chapter 3: Type One - The Perfectionist

The Type One or Perfectionist personality type is the first to be covered as the description of this personality is quite self-explanatory. As it is referred to in the late Riso's book, *Personality Types: Using the Enneagram for Self-Discovery*, those individuals who match this personality as they will be referred to as One's are never happy until things are perfect in their eyes.

Ones will never accept any flaws from themselves, and from others, and from any situation. They are always stressing about how to constantly improve anything that they encounter. Their way of thinking is idealistic whenever it comes to putting chaos in order which they cannot accept that it rarely can be done. Or if it can be done, it will not happen in a timely manner. And even though it is always admirable to have the desire to keep improving and becoming the best versions of oneself, the Ones take it to the extreme. They take it to the level that is clearly unattainable.

Each time they find that a goal they have made for themselves is unattainable, then they become guilty that they failed as failure is not an option for Ones. And when they are guilty, they become angry, and then they become guilty of being angry. This guilt and anger cycle becomes a vicious one, and this is a cycle that cannot be broken by the Perfectionist type.

It is clear that no one is harder on them other than themselves. If they get something wrong or if they miss points for anything they work hard to do, then they will berate themselves for not being good enough. They cannot handle just not getting it 'right' whatever it may be. They have a very difficult time relaxing and don't understand how to enjoy the small pleasures in life. They are too anxious, stressed, and too occupied with the ideas of perfection in every situation in order to find joy, and they almost never laugh either.

One's personality type would have emerged in early childhood. Even as early as a year old when they stumbled while learning to walk. They would have gotten very upset over tumbling over other toddlers that are of other personality types. And as they had matured and grown, while they gained more awareness, their perfectionist style became more prominent when they started going to school.

If they had difficulty with reading or doing a math problem, they would not be able to accept that they were struggling. They would have been the types to call themselves stupid and other names, which in the end would have been damaging to their self-esteem. That also meant that these types would have been upset over getting a 99 percent mark on a test or an assignment because it did not reach that 100 mark. Other personality types would have been thrilled to have gotten a high mark; they would have been thrilled to have aced the test or the assignment. But not the Ones.

The same applied whenever it came to friendships. Especially if they wanted to become friends or even develop a relationship with someone who they were fond of and were turned down. They would ruminate about what they could have done to repel the individual that they were fond of and would then berate themselves for not being perfect, and likable. They could never understand that sometimes a lack of chemistry is the reason that friendships and relationships don't work out. They take full responsibility for it.

However, the positive traits the Ones are known to have is that they are responsible, organized, hard-working, and are list-makers, and very loyal. They also follow the rules carefully and expect others to follow the rules as well. This now brings this to covering how Ones behave in the workplace as well as the type of occupations that are the most fitting for this personality type. In the next section of this chapter, the way Ones are in the workplace will be covered.

Ones In The Workplace

According to what is written about the Ones in the workplace based on what is written in the late Riso's book, *Personality Types: Using the Enneagram for Self-Discovery*, there is no doubt at all based on the serious nature that they take their jobs seriously. In fact, Ones are known to be workaholics and will refuse to go back home until all of their tasks at work are completed - perfectly. And they will come back home being anxious about whether or not they had done a good job with their work as they would be nervous about how the boss will respond to their efforts - and they will constantly think about the feedback.

In fact, they will keep worrying about the boss' feedback about their performance at work is less than perfect and this will literally keep them up at night. That also means that because they are extremely serious and have an incredible amount of self-control and self-discipline when it comes to their work and anything else they do in their lives, they are naturally industrious, take the rules seriously, they are practical, they are organized and are the ideal employee for any company to have. That is because the Ones are guaranteed to do a fantastic job, regardless of how they feel about it which will likely be not good enough since that is within their nature to not take pride in any work they do. That is clearly because it is far from perfect.

However, even though they are the ideal employee for any company, type Ones would only thrive in these particular types of jobs which are:

- Financial Planning

- Banking

- Blogging

- Writing

- Property Management

- Any Manager

- Attorney

- Accountant

- Professor

- Scientist

- Technician

- Welder

- Artist

- Any Type of CEO

As much as the Ones are natural born followers when it comes to the rules, they are also natural-born leaders. However, only a few personality types would be able to work under the Perfectionist manager. Other Ones would clash with them terribly. And, Ones would make excellent managers as far as making sure that the employees that they are managing get the work done perfectly and in a timely manner.

That also makes you wonder how Ones would be

able to manage relationships of any kind since they not only expect perfection from themselves but expect it from others. That is considering that they would put a lot of pressure on anyone who they end up having any kind of relationship with. That means anyone who they are in a personal relationship with, or friends, or co-workers. Before that is looked into, the types of jobs that the Ones are not ideal for will give you an idea of how their personal relationships would be. The types of jobs that the Ones are better off avoiding are:

- Teaching Kindergarten or elementary school-aged children

- Comedy Improv

- Doctors

- Nursing

- Bartending

- Waiting

- Or any job that requires them to deal with people on a regular basis except for those they work with.

That is why the Ones make good managers and CEOs. And in the last section of this chapter, the types of relationships they end up with, as well as the struggles will be covered.

Ones And Relationships

Because of the fact that Ones expect as much perfection out of others as much as they do of themselves, they would have a difficult time maintaining relationships. And many of them end up in divorce for these traits as well. That is because they are not compassionate and expect their partners to follow the rules and they always put them high up on a pedestal which they always fall from in the end. That is when the relationships with the Ones become sour. That goes for marriage, dating, friendships, and any relationships that they would form with co-workers.

In fact, many of the One's co-workers would not want to work with them because they would feel uncomfortable and bullied by them since they will be judged harshly. And, many of the co-workers would do what they can to avoid them. However, other co-workers that are Ones would clash and would even get into heated arguments.

Even though the Ones appear that they are the types that would not able to have a relationship with anyone because of their judgmental and highly analytical nature, there are personality types that would be able to maintain a relationship with the Ones. More information on that will be covered later on in this eBook. That is because even though Ones expect perfection and are very hard on those who they are in relationships with, they are still extremely loyal, take their relationships seriously, and are extremely honest which are traits that are extremely desirable and respectable.

However, Ones can make difficult parents as well as they would put a lot of expectations on their kids and could unintentionally cause their kids to have anxiety about getting things done correctly. Their kids at school would be afraid to show them a test that they had failed or did not do well on because of knowing that their Type One parent would react angrily towards them. They would also fall into the authoritarian parenting style which means they control every aspect of their children's lives. That will only cause their children to have low self-esteem or become rebellious and not want to have anything to do with their Type One as they become older and more independent.

Many Type One Parents would also not be able to accept a child with special needs because of the fact that in their eyes, a child with a disability would be less than perfect. However, there would be some Type One parents that would accept the child with a disability if they saw the potential for the child to do well later on and would work tirelessly with them to help them get to that point.

To sum up about the Type One - Perfectionist, those who have this personality type are what their type is labeled as which has a perfectionist way of thinking. They expect themselves to be perfect and are constantly improving themselves to the point of obsession. They also expect the same from others whether it is their mates, their peer, their friends, their co-workers, and kids. Yet at the same time, they are also quite loyal, honest, dependable, hard-working, and organized. The Ones are very different from the next personality type of the Enneagram structure, which is the Type Two - The Helper.

The next chapter will cover every aspect of The Helper personality type.

Chapter 4: Type Two - The Helper

The Type Two or The Helper, as the late Riso had stated in his book, *Personality Types: Using the Enneagram for Self-Discovery*, is the type to be there for anyone to help them because that is exactly what they are - helpers. They are there at any time for anyone in need. They are extremely selfless and put their needs last. They are all about love, and they are the types that would remember the birthdays and anniversaries of others whether they are family members, co-workers, acquaintances or friends.

They are extremely warm and caring and are very emotional. Their homes are always welcome to others and will be the first to cook up a hearty meal to anyone in need. And this trait would be seen in early childhood. Children don't normally develop empathy until they are in grade 3 or 4 because they are only aware of themselves and are only aware of their own needs before that.

However, the Twos have shown empathy even at a very young age. Even as babies they would have shown empathy of some sort by snuggling up to any of their caregivers and giving them a kiss on the cheek to the best of their ability.

As toddlers, Twos would give plenty of hugs and would have shown love to animals and even to younger babies. As children, they would have begged their parents for a pet to cuddle and they would also be kind of their younger siblings. As the Twos became older and started going to school, they would also be the first to befriend anyone. Especially the underdog. And they may have been the underdog as well which would have increased their empathetic feelings for those who also had an obvious rough time.

Twos most definitely spend a lot of their energy caring for the needs of others, and the trap that they can easily fall into is becoming burned out by putting their needs last. And whenever that happens to anyone, they learn the hard way that they cannot pour out of an empty cup. However, you would think that the Twos based on their traits would be the ultimate saints. You would think that they are giving and caring without expecting anything back from anyone because from what you had just read, that appears to be their nature.

The Twos may be selfless, caring, empathetic, and are there to put the needs of others first before them. However, they don't do it without any ulterior motives. They expect to be appreciated and expect others to give back as well by appreciating them. They don't expect to be given material gifts, but if they feel at all that they are being taken for granted, they will not let that go. They expect you to thank them in a genuine way. They will expect that you have them over for dinner or dessert as well to thank them for their kindness and selflessness. They want to be needed, and they want to help, but it comes with a cost.

In fact, if they feel that they are not being appreciated and are not given back what they had given out, they can become abusive, irrational, and quite hysterical. As long as they feel that they have been compensated for their efforts in the ways that satisfied them, they will continue to be there for others to help in any way possible.

They would not expect to be given back what they had given out to those who they know are not capable of doing so or are quite incapacitated such as caring for animals, babies and young children, the elderly, the ill, and the disabled whether it would be physical or mental. That is because the Twos know that those in this group cannot give back and they genuinely help those in this group because again, they love to be needed and those that fall in this category are naturally dependent.

They would also give a free pass to those who are in an authoritative position such as a parent or even more so their bosses. They know that they have to be at their best with their bosses. However, if they are happy with what they are earning at work, then they will be happy to give more to their bosses. If their bosses are asking them to do tasks that the Twos do not feel compensated for on a constant basis, then they will start to look for another job behind their backs.

However, when it comes to fully functional adults as well as older children and teenagers, they will expect them to show their appreciation towards them for their efforts. Otherwise, they will not be kind and will become quite nasty towards them. They expect to receive the same love that they had given to others, and the reason behind this ulterior motive that the Twos have is because if they are not given back the love they had given and are not appreciated- then it blemished their self-image. This is a huge threat to them. This is why they become abusive, irritational and inconsolable.

Other than that, because of the ultimate giving nature, they will only work in jobs that are fitting for their personality type. In the next section, the description of their ideal jobs and how they behave in the workplace will be covered.

Twos In The Workplace

The late Riso had stated in his book, Personality Types: Using the Enneagram for Self-Discovery that the Twos are all about helping others and wanting to be needed by others, even with their ulterior motive. The way the Twos would behave in the workplace would be no different from any other setting.

A typical day at work for the Type Two would be leaving home to head to work. And if he or she is driving and sees that a driver on the other lane wants to pass, of course, the Two would slow down and allow the driver to pass because again, anyone else's needs are put ahead of their own. And if the driver thanks the Two by using the hand gesture that indicates a thank you, then the Two will be happy to have received that kind gesture from the driver on the road.

If the driver, however, does not thank the Two,

then the Two will become aggressive by honking at the driver that he or she allowed to pass, or even worse, giving the driver the finger and screaming profanities even though the other driver wouldn't hear it. Maybe the Two would even go as far as purposely tailgating the driver. Either way, the Two would expect to be thanked even on the way to work or anywhere else they are going.

And, once the Two type goes to the office, he or she will begin to start working as expected. However, it will be a matter of time that a co-worker is in need of some help for some reason. Perhaps they had run out of paper and are unsure of where to look for extra paper or other supplies. The Two will immediately stop what he or she is doing and will go out of his or her way to help the co-worker find the paper or the supplies that are needed. More often than not, the co-worker will thank the Two type, and that will be enough for the Two to get back to work because of being satisfied for being thanked for his or her efforts in regard to helping the co-worker find the supplies needed.

If the co-worker doesn't thank the Two type properly, then he or she will become angry and will be simmering. Because of the fact that he or she knows to behave at work in order to keep the job, the Type Two will not scream and yell at the co-worker for the lack of appreciation. Instead, he or she will display passive-aggressive behaviors towards the ungrateful co-worker such as being extremely sarcastic. And the co-worker would not understand why the Type Two was being incredibly nasty and did not realize that the explanation for the nasty treatment was due to not showing appreciation for The Helper's efforts.

And, what would end up happening is that The Helper would simmer about not being shown appreciation and allow it to fester all day at work, and on the way home. This is where the Twos would get into trouble when it comes to their work environment. If they do not feel appreciated by their co-workers for something, they went out of their way to do, then they become angry and allow their intense irate feelings fester. That means the quality of their work would suffer due to being too distracted from being angry about the fact that they were taken for granted, which they believe.

That means in order for the Twos to perform well at the job, they have to feel that any of their co-workers that they had gone out of their way to help appreciated them for their efforts. Otherwise, their sour feelings towards their ungrateful co-workers would hurt their performance.

Aside from that, the type of careers that the Twos are best suited for since they are extremely people-oriented are:

- Providing therapy

- Teaching

- Doctor

- Nurse

- Sales

- Bartending

- Waiting

- Publishing

- Advice Columnist

- Matchmaking

- Writing

And, the Twos are happy to provide as much as they can to others in the work they do because they are being paid. That is the compensation they need, and they don't need their patie4nts or clients to thank them for their hard work if they are getting paid.

The types of jobs the Twos must avoid are:

- Editor

- Tax agent

- Agent

- Officer

- Admissions for college

Now you know how the Twos are in a working environment. In the final section of this chapter, the way their relationships end up will be covered more in-depth than how it has previously.

Twos And Their Relationships

Twos will do anything to make sure that the needs of their lovers, their friends, and as stated above, their co-workers are met. However, there is an ulterior motive. That is because they have to feel appreciated for their selfless duties and for the sacrifices they have made for them. If not, then they became abusive, irrational, and end up in hysterics.

The lack of compensation threatens their core and their self-image reflects literally the type that they are - The Helper. They want to help but expect to be thanked. When their children are little, they will not expect anything back from them because of the fact that they are not capable of giving back. However, as their children age and mature, that changes.

The Twos will eventually expect to be appreciated by their own children once they are old enough to understand how to give back. In fact, many teenage and adult children of the Twos end up cutting them out because of how their parents really don't give of themselves of the goodness of their hearts. The only times that the Twos will not place any expectations on children if they have special needs.

Yet that also depends on the severity of the disability as well. If the child is mildly disabled whether it is mental or physical, the same demands will be placed on that child as they would be on their typical siblings. If the disability is severe or profound, then they will not be expected to give back because they cannot.

It would also not be surprising to learn that many Twos end up in failed marriages because of their expectations and demands for being appreciated. Many friends that they had would have also given up on them for the fact that they are too demanding and may even find the Twos quite draining. The Twos suffer at work as well as in relationships of all kinds.

The next personality type of the Enneagram is the Type 3 - The Performer who will be covered in the following chapter.

Chapter 5: Type 3 - The Performer

The third personality type that is talked about in many sources which include the late Riso's book, *Personality Types: Using the Enneagram for Self-Discovery*, is the Type Three personality or The Performer. If you think that the performer has a knack for performing music or anything that is related, that could be fitting - as long as they are the cream of the crop.

The Threes or the Performers are also known as the Achievers. And if you now have a better idea of what personality type they are, and you have guessed that they are constantly improving their performance no matter what it may be in because as long as they are successful, then they are happy - you are right.

The Threes are constantly upping their game only to be successful. And it can be anything from being them being the best-looking person around with that perfectly toned body in their social circle or them becoming a millionaire or just the best at anything that is important to them that they do. The frequently compare their success to others, and they are highly competitive because they will not accept anything other than reaching the top.

This personality type may sound like it is parallel to the Ones, and to some degree it is. The difference is that the Ones are just obsessed with perfection in general. They aren't particularly looking to be the best-looking individual or the wealthiest around per se. The Ones just want to have everything in their lives perfect because they can't rest if there is any disorganization or disarray which causes perfection. They feel like the ultimate failures if they don't achieve perfection, and they are not gregarious.

The Threes, however, aren't looking for perfection per se other than then being the best in what they do, and they are actually quite gregarious and extroverted. For instance, the

Ones would become upset if the house was not clean and organized because that means the house is not in tip top perfect shape. The Threes would not be concerned about that unless they were striving to become the best housekeepers. In other words, the Threes are only looking for perfection when it comes to their own achievements, not when it comes to anything else.

That means that the Threes are constantly bettering their performance in anything that is important to them so they can attain success. That is what is validating to their self-image. As long as they are successful in whatever it is that is important to them, then they feel secure. They also are quite likable which was already mentioned, they are charismatic, and are the types that are known to be the most popular at school.

This personality type is also seen from early childhood once they begin to gain awareness. The Threes really start to stand out when they start school, even as early as kindergarten. If they are given an art project to do, they would have done anything they could to make their artwork stand out better than the artwork created by their classmates. And if any of their classmates did a better job than they did, then that would have upset the Threes to the core - even in kindergarten.

As the Threes matured and evolved throughout school, then that would apply to them being the best at sports. In fact, if they were playing baseball during a physical education session, not only would they have insisted that their team won - but they would have insisted on being the reason that their baseball team won. The Threes had to be the ones to achieve that winning home run or else they would feel like the ultimate loser, and that means they would feel invalidated. Even if their baseball team at school had won.

The same goes for them having the need to be the most popular kid at school, and the best-looking, and the one to be able to get the boy or girl of their dreams to date. Not all Threes in school cared about getting the best grades if that was not at all important to them, and that is also what makes this personality type different from the Ones. That would only apply to the Threes that cared about being the best of their class academically, and in that case, they would strive to become the valedictorian. For the Threes that care about being the best performers academically, and did not make it to the valedictorian status, they would feel like the ultimate failure and loser.

Threes appear to be confident because they are quite extroverted and usually dress quite well, even if they are not concerned about being the prettiest or the most handsome person around. However, they are actually extremely insecure and are afraid to become intimate because that means they would end up exposing their vulnerabilities if they were. No matter how much success the Threes have achieved, it will not be good enough because every failure they encountered sticks to them. That means if they were intimate, then their past failures could be seen which is the last thing that they want to see happen.

If the Threes feel threatened in any way by any type of competition, they become ruthless, narcissistic, and will not care who gets hurt as long as they attain their goals- and beat their competition. Their sense of morals would disappear and would be happy to throw anyone under the bus for whatever reason.

Here is a scenario. A Three is a master internet marketer and partnered up with someone who is well-known in the internet marketing community to create an elite course on SEO. The Three had intended to make this course the cream of the crop- better than the ones out there! And, the intention was to have the course launched by a certain date if that meant that a competitor was going to be releasing a similar course around the same time. That meant the course had to be released well before the competitor was going to release their course in SEO.

A date was chosen, and the partner of the Three had to be present during the time of the release. However, on the day of the release, the partner had gotten sick, or one of the family members had to be taken to the hospital. This meant the partner was not going to be able to be present during the release date. This meant having to delay the release of the course. The Three would not stand for that because that would mean the competitor would end up releasing their SEO course before the Three did.

That means the Three would release the course anyway behind the partner's back and would end up taking all of the credit instead of even acknowledging the partner's expertise in SEO. This had to happen so the course would be released long before the competitor had released theirs. The Three would not care whether or not the partner had a personal emergency to tend to which was the reason that the course had to be delayed. The Three had to win because that was the only way that his or her self-image could be protected. If the competitor's course had come out before the Three's did, and if others found it to be quite valuable, then they would have no need to purchase Three's course - and the worst could happen as well!

The competitor could potentially end up as the master in SEO because his or her course was released first. That would not be acceptable to the Three.

You have an idea of how the Three would behave in the workplace which will be covered more in detail in the next section of this chapter.

Threes In The Workplace

It is quite easy to imagine how competitive the Three type would be among co-workers. They have to be the employee of the month each and every month and will do anything possible to make that happen. That even means them telling their bosses the things that their co-workers did to get them into trouble in order to make sure that they are the employees of the month. That also would mean that if they remained as their boss' favorite employee, then they would be the first ones chosen to receive a promotion.

After all, that is what the Threes want. They want to keep climbing up the corporate ladder. They want to keep striving for betterment only so they truly are considered as the best of the best. Failure is not an option, because if a peer or a co-worker outperforms the Three, then that will cause the Performer to feel like the ultimate loser. That is something that cannot be handled at all costs.

That means that working with a Three type co-worker would be a nightmare. The Three would be the type to bully him or her if she or he was a threat to the Three's success in any way at all. The Threes would also be the best fitting for certain job types and would not a poor fit for other jobs.

The list of careers that best fit the type Three are:

- Producer

- News or any type of journalist

- Disk jockey

- Attorney

- Literary agent

- Sports agent

- Entertainer

- Beauty-related

- Author

- Internet marketer (because it is competitive)

The worst types of jobs would be for the Threes are:

- Freelance writing since there is no need to strive to be the top of the competition

- Running an Etsy store or being self-employed that does not encourage career advancement

In fact, the Threes would do poorly when it comes to any type of free-form career advancement because they have nothing to show off. If they do better with their own businesses and no one would know the difference, then that is not validating enough to them to see themselves as successful.

This also means Threes would struggle when it comes to their personal relationships which include family which will be covered in the next chapter.

Threes And Relationships

If you have guessed that the Three- type personality would struggle to maintain relationships, then you are right because of the fact that they are afraid to be intimate. That means they make themselves vulnerable to anyone. They don't ever want to show their failures or insecurities in general to anyone. Especially if the Three is extremely concerned about their own body image and they don't want to expose their less-than-perfect parts of their bodies to anyone.

However, for the Threes that aren't concerned about their body image may have a little bit of an easier time being intimate and forming relationships. It all depends on the area that the Threes care about advancing. Unfortunately, many of them end up in failed marriages or relationships. That is because if the Three received a promotion from work which meant an opportunity for them to move out of town to advance their career- and their significant other had held them back, then the Three would rather throw the relationship away than pass up that golden opportunity to help them validate themselves.

Here is a scenario. The Three was married to someone who had a sick parent to tend to which meant that the spouse was constantly taking the parent to doctor's appointments. The Three also had received an opportunity through work to advance the career which meant the family had to relocate. However, the spouse could not consider leaving the city at the time because of having to care for the sick parent. The spouse might have another concern about that as well, which is the worry about not finding a job so quickly if the relocation happened. The Three would not stand for that and would file for divorce and take off anyway.

This means that advancing their career is so important to them that family comes second. The Three would also even consider leaving the kids behind with the spouse in this situation as well if the kids held them back.

Speaking of kids, the Three's kids would have a difficult time meeting his or her approval. That is because the Performer expects success not just from him or herself, but from the kids. It is not uncommon for children of the Three-type to cut themselves off from the Performer parent when they reach adulthood for this reason. Their kids would refer them to as being narcissistic and toxic parents. That would also mean that if the Three had a child with special needs, then that in itself would be the ultimate failure.

Producing a less-than-perfect child would be scarring to the Three's self-image and would not even consider working with the child. The Three would likely want to give the child up for adoption or to surrender the child to the state and would want to forget about the fact that the child was even born. This is just another example of how the Three could be ruthless if their self-image was at the risk of being tarnished.

When it comes to friendships, the Threes would have a difficult time maintaining friendships as well if they had held their opportunities for success back in any way. This is quite apparent that attaining and achieving success is more important than personal relationships.

The next personality type in the Enneagram model that will be covered in the next chapter is the Type 4 - The Romantic.

Chapter 6: Type 4- The Romantic

The Type Four personality or The Romantic as it is stated in the late Riso's book, *Personality Types: Using the Enneagram for Self-Discovery*, is also referred to as The Individualist. Fours are known to be extremely creative, idealistic, very empathetic, and make their unique selves known. They are also nonconformist.

In fact, they create their own identities based on their own perceptions of being different from the rest. They see their differences from others as both a good thing and a bad thing. They see it as a positive thing because they do not like to be considered as clones or as sheep. However, the negative thing about this aspect is that Fours often feel that they are unable to feel the same types of pleasures and happiness that others feel from common things.

Examples of those are enjoying the simple things

such as a sunny day, a freshly brewed cup of coffee, or a glass of wine. It is not that Fours don't enjoy those things, but they get a lot more enjoyment from anything that is more complex. It frustrates them that they cannot experience the same kind of pleasure that others experience from the simple things in life.

That being said, Fours realize they are complex beings, and they consider that to be both a blessing and a curse. They suffer from both a superiority and an inferiority complex. They think that they are both "better" than others, but at the same time, they envy others for a variety of reasons.

They think they are superior over others because of the fact that they are not a clone like most people are. However, they long for the simpler lives that people live. In fact, their feelings towards others go from feeling superior over them feeling shameful and defective compared to them. As it is said, Fours are extremely complex.

They often feel misunderstood which adds to their frustration and have a strong desire to be understood, which they feel they never are, and quite often they feel unappreciated. They are extremely moody, temperamental, can be quite melodramatic and melancholic. They have a tendency to withdraw from others and stay in their own world. Their own world is the only place that makes sense to them. Their own place in their heads is the only place where they can seek sanctuary because the real world is cold and crude which they cannot be a part of because it is extremely overwhelming, and their hearts cannot take it.

Fours also badly miss people and situations that failed to work out for them and fantasize about those people or situations coming back. They fantasize about the future as well. They do this to escape in general. This aspect is what also makes the Four type personality quite empathetic.

Fours are extremely sensitive and have a soft spot for the underdog, for the weak, and for animals.

They are prone to mental illness such as depression and addiction because they are constantly looking for external ways to bring them relief from their chronic inner woes. They can easily drink, eat, and do drugs and become addicted to all of it. Some, unfortunately, engage in self-harm such as cutting and can easily develop eating disorders.

The Romantic types are the ones that will easily express their feelings through forms of art such as painting, drawing, writing, music, and many of them are into body art. Those who are inked and have plenty of piercings are likely Fours because that is how they express their individualistic selves.

The Fours are also likely to be interested in unusual genres of music, television, books, and movies. They will only like a common genre of any of it if a particular song, show, movie, or book relates to them in any way. For instance, the average Four would scoff at chick flick movies or light-hearted comedies but would love to watch a farce, offbeat comedy movie such as the 1995 flick, *Four Rooms* that was directed by Quentin Tarantino.

They would also be likely to detest any type of pop music that is in the top 40 because it represents what everyone else likes. They would be drawn more towards genres such as thrash metal, punk, alternative, ambient, and house music. Any genre that represents uniqueness, just like who they are.

This personality type would show their individualistic side ever since early childhood as they would be the type to play with a spoon or an object as opposed to a common toy that other kids would like. They are the ones who likely were bullied and picked on during their school years because of being so different. They would respond by withdrawing more and going into their own safe world. They would have had the most difficult time during their middle school years until the end of high school.

Fours would have both been likely to be disgusted by the popular crowd because of them being clones, yet at the same time would have been envious for them for having such easy lives - as they had perceived.

Depending on how the Fours would have responded to their bullies, they would have either drowned more into their sorrows and could have ended up ending up at a very bad place - or they would have rebelled and told them off in their own way by continuing to be themselves and by going into their faces.

Based on the idealistic type and individualistic type of The Romantic, you would assume that the Fours would not end up working at any conventional job. In the next section of this chapter, the Fours and the workplace will be covered more in depth.

Fours In The Workplace

If you had guessed that the Fours would not

mesh well in conventional workplace settings, that guess is right. Fours would be quite miserable in a typical 9 to 5 work environment. As it was previously mentioned, Fours are idealistic and do not always think in practical terms that they would need to work in a company that is stable in order to earn the money they need to survive.

Many Fours become artists as they rely on art in order to express themselves as many are creative writers, musicians, and artists of other types. The problem with that is that money may not be made at all by relying on those unstable career types.

Even though that is the case, most Fours do realize they need to have a steady job of some sort as they are in reality enough to know they have to earn some kind of reliable income to get by. They need money to eat, to pay rent or a mortgage if they actually were fortunate enough to buy a home or a condo, and they need to pay for their utility expenses. However, they still hope to become successful musicians, artists, or writers one day. And they would only work in the following types of more or less reliable jobs in order to survive:

- Hairstyling

- Manicurist

- Pedicurist

- Salon worker

- Tattoo artist

- Yoga teacher

- Therapist, because they can relate to those who are struggling with their mental health, and can find a way to help them

- Masseuse

- Reflexologist

- Acupuncturist

- Creative writing instructor

- A clerk at a New Age store

- Graphic designer

- Freelance writer

- Internet marketer

- Marketing and advertising without selling personally

- Content creation for social media managers

- Entrepreneur because they would be excellent marketers and could easily brand themselves in a unique way

They readily take on roles of those jobs while they work on the side writing a book, creating music, or doing artwork on the side. They still fantasize that they would be best-sellers one day, or highly popular musicians or successful artists. However, most Fours do realize that they need to have a stable job as the ones that are the most fitting in order to live.

The worst possible jobs that the Fours could end up falling into are:

- Any kind of 9 to 5 job at any office

- Anything administrative

- Police officer

- Stockbroker

- Accounting

- Law

- Medicine

- Any job that has to be based on the rules or standards of someone else

The only exception to this is if they were hired by a company as a marketer or advertiser that has nothing to do with sales. They would come up with the creative marketing ideas so that a sales representative could use.

Based on all that has been said, Fours would not

mix well with other co-workers as they only want to work alone unless they are serving clients in job roles that are the most suitable to them which was mentioned above.

You may also wonder if the Fours are complete loners that would never want to get married, let alone to be in a relationship; however, that is not always the case. The last section of this chapter will cover Fours and their relationship types.

Fours And Relationships

Based on what you would have learned about The Romantic type is that they would never want to be in a relationship at all. Because of their extreme individualistic nature, they would be the type to live a solo life and have the freedom to do what they want while they are living in a studio apartment. However, that is not always the case.

Many Fours actually do want to be in relationships, and that only has to do with the fact that they would become lonely if they did not have a mate. It is true that they would not want to be in a relationship because of society's expectations. They want to be with partners for the sake of not being alone for the rest of their lives. And, they would be quite picky with who they would be in a relationship with.

They would not want to hook up with someone who was concerned with meeting society's standards. In other words, they would not want to be in a relationship with anyone who would not have a mind of their own. Fours are naturally not attracted to clones. They would only hook up with those who embraced their own unique ways and rebelled towards society's expectations. That is the most attractive trait that the Fours are looking for which goes for them looking for their life partners as well as the friends they want to make.

Fours may be individualistic, but they still need human interaction. Many are hermits and only socialize on their own terms. And many of them do get married because that is what they want for their own reasons, not for pleasing anyone else. Many Fours also go and have kids of their own, and they are the ones that teach their kids to embrace their uniqueness. They will teach their kids to follow their hearts and not to allow themselves to be pressured by anyone else in life.

And, as much as Fours detest rules in general, they will tell their kids to respect elders and to be respectful towards others because it is the right thing to do. Morals are morals and Fours want their kids to have morals and to be kind. Fours would also likely be able to nurture a child with special needs properly because they naturally are empathetic towards the underdog in general. They would teach a child with exceptional needs on how to embrace themselves in their best ability.

Fours are idealistic, nonconforming, highly creative, extremely emotional, and only want to engage with others that are also quite individualistic. They are also once again attracted to the underdog and will have a lot of sympathy and empathy towards those who have lived colorful and harsh lives. They detest society and its standards and will not have anything to do with those who are seen as popular or who have had a life that did not present them a lot of challenges. The next personality type that will be covered in the following chapter is The Type 5 personality, which is The Investigator.

Chapter 7: Type 5 - The Investigator

Those who are in the Type Five group or the ones who are referred to as The Investigator type have some similarities to the Fours but are also quite different. As the late Riso had stated in his book, *Personality Types: Using the Enneagram for Self-Discovery*, Fives are those who observe, gain knowledge and wisdom through observing and experiences. However, they keep themselves. They keep away from human interaction because they do not want to be part of the drama at any cost.

Fives are known to be extremely analytical, private, unobtrusive, self-sufficient, and are very thoughtful. They spend their lives gaining knowledge as well as wisdom. Those who are in the Investigator group are quite independent, objective, are the types to be calm when it comes to any kind of crises, and they are highly intelligent because they are always very busy taking in information.

However, as observant and as intelligent as they are, the Fives are quite detached and finds ways to protect themselves from those that can pose some kind of risk to them or from those who may end up asking too much. They also come off as quite eccentric, indifferent, they never want to intrude or be in anyone's way at all which even means they will suffer in silence and are withdrawn and shy.

That means even if they genuinely needed someone's help, they would not want to ask for it due to the fear that they would be obtrusive. This even includes medical emergencies unless it is a matter of life and death, then they would know they would not have a choice but to go to the ER or to their doctor. Otherwise, they would rather find a way to heal themselves even though they may not be in the medical field themselves. But since they are the types to have the constant hunger to learn, they would spend time researching how to heal an illness or a condition that does not necessarily need the help of a doctor.

The one thing that the Fives want more than anything is to understand the reasons behind everything, how things work and are the types to want to be able to give the right answer to any question that is asked. They are extremely terrified deep down from being helpless and incompetent. In fact, they are incredibly sensitive. And in order to mask this sensitive side, they make it known that they are indifferent and will not hesitate to show off their intellect. They also know their social skills are weak and they show off their smarts to overcompensate for that truth. That means the Fives can easily become intellectually arrogant which will only repel others, which is what they want anyway since they have no time or patience for human interaction.

The Investigator personality would show up in early childhood. The youngster would show immediate interest in learning even as older infants. Even though babies are naturally curious as it is because they are learning about the world around them, the Fives would show an intense interest in learning during toddlerhood by constantly looking at age-appropriate books, as well as having the need to solve age-appropriate puzzles and stacking toys.

They also would not have any desire to play with other kids or parallel play. This may alarm parents because these are the traits that professionals look for that can be indicative of an autism spectrum disorder such as Asperger's Syndrome. However, not all Fives are on the spectrum, as many neurotypical individuals possess the Investigator personality.

Once the Fives enter kindergarten and are in early grade school, their thirst and hunger for learning become more intense. They will want to borrow books from the library that will offer them something intellectual to read and to stay so they can gain knowledge. They have no time for fiction or fantasy books because they are not learning anything from reading those books and it does not stimulate their intellect. Any kind of fiction that the Fives accept is Sci-Fi. That keeps their brains stimulated.

The Fives have always been the type during childhood to read a book, or even get a head start on doing homework while sitting in a corner by themselves during recess. While the other kids are outside playing with each other, the Fives keep to themselves. The Investigator would be known as that straight-A student and as the teacher's pet. In later elementary school, and during junior high, they would become targets of bullying because of this, and the other kids would call them nerds or geeks.

When the Fives enter high school, this trait becomes even more intense as they keep maturing. At that point, they could be bullied even more viciously because of the fact that not only are they considered as the nerds, but their peers would pick up on the eccentricities that the Fives possess.

That also means that because the Fives come off as eccentric, unfeeling, and are only concerned with tools such as books, computers, or anything else to feed their brains - they actually have a lot more feelings underneath that outer shell that is projected. They have some similar traits to the Fours, however, unlike the Fours, Fives are not comfortable with expressing themselves in any way at all whereas the Fours do with body art, or through painting, writing, or through music. Fives would prefer to disappear from the world if they had a choice in order to not make themselves known at all.

Fives have an easier time socially at university because of the fact that they will go into a field such as medicine, science, engineering and anything else that requires more devotion to the study rather than with human interaction. They will be placed in classes with peers that are studying the same field, which means it is likely that many of their classmates are Fives as well and would keep to themselves as a result.

If you are wondering how Fives interact at work, and what the best career choices are, that will be covered in the next section of this chapter.

Fives In The Workplace

It would not come to anyone as a surprise that the typical Five would work in any field that is the most fitting for their type alone and behind the scenes. They really don't want to be seen and intrude in any way at all. That means Fives will not be at all suitable for any type of office environment and would not work a typical 9 to 5 job at all. In fact, the best types of career-roles for the Fives are:

- Engineering

- Anything to do with technology

- Game and app design

- Researcher

- Analyst

- Scientist

- Mathematician

- Astronomer

- Lab technician

- Professor (only when it comes to teaching university students fields in any of the above listed)

Fives have the capacity and interest to go into medicine. However, they would not make good doctors because that means they have to interact and treat patients. However, they could possibly become pharmacists which means they will still have to interact with patients picking up prescriptions. Though the level of interaction they would have with people is reduced.

The worst career-choices for Fives are:

- Any field that requires them to interact with people

- Publicist

- Hospitality

- Retail

- Waiting

- Bartending

- Teaching high school and elementary school

- Childcare

Many Fives like animals but they would also not become veterinarians because of having to deal with pet owners. However, if their dealings with people were limited, some may agree to become veterinary technicians if they happen to have a strong interest in animals.

At the same time, Fives would not care about the niche they would work in if they had an engineering job that meant they would be behind the scenes. For instance, many Fives work as engineers at radio stations, a setting where there is a lot of human interaction whether it would be by the phone or those in the area visiting the radio announcers. Fives don't care about that as long as they are away from people while working with the machinery.

Here is another example of what form of work setting is ideal for the majority of Fives. Fives that are scientists, engineers, or technicians would grab at the chance to winter over at a remote setting such as Concordia Station in Antarctica which is literally out in the middle of nowhere. The weather is the most severe in this area as well, especially during the long and very dark winter. They would have to work with those in the same setting as them in that particular building. However, they usually don't have a problem with that since those who they are working with are likely other Fives and will only socialize when it suits them.

That means you would also wonder based on what was said about the Fives that they would be complete hermits since they avoid social contact at all costs. However, this is not always the case. More about Fives and relationships will be covered in the last section of this chapter.

Fives And Relationships

Based on what has been covered on the Fives, people may think of them as hermits that spend their entire lives studying, reading intellectually stimulating books for the rest of their lives. However, the fact of the matter is that one of the basic needs for everyone regardless of their personality type is engaging in social interaction. Even the Fives themselves are aware of this. The complete lack of social interaction can induce mental illnesses and other illnesses. It is a basic need, just as how clothing, food, water, and shelter are.

Fives will also not close themselves off if they happen to come across those who are just like them. If they come across another Investigator type, then they will let go of the insecurities of their poor social skills and actually be confident enough to be themselves. That is because if they come across anyone who is just like themselves, then they can be free. There is nothing preventing them from being closed-off. Think back to that example of the scientists and technicians hanging out with one another at the remote Antarctic Concordia Station.

When Fives connect with those who are just like themselves, there is no worry about the lack of understanding and any threat that is perceived due to being around other people disappears. When you have a group of Fives together in one room, then they will hang together, and watch Sci-Fi movies, and laugh and joke around with one another. They don't care that their sense of humor would be considered off-beat because the others around them would completely appreciate it. And, yes, that means, Fives actually do have a sense of humor, but it never comes out unless they are in a setting with other Fives.

The thing about friendships and Fives is that

once the Investigator makes a friend, then that friend is one for life. Many Fives have also gotten married and have had children. They would only connect with those who were just like them, just as the Fours would.

However, once Fives do get married and have children, the problems they could run into are when their kids begin to go to school. This means their kids parents, the Investigators, will need to be interacting with the teachers. Especially when problems arise, and that is a guarantee at some point.

Fives as parents may discourage their kids from being part of any kind of group because that is how they are. This could be a disservice to their kids, especially if their kids are more extraverted. However, Fives will stress the importance of making a good lifelong friend as long as the right type of friend is connected.

You have learned a lot about the Fives in this chapter. In the next chapter, the next personality type in the Enneagram model will be covered. That is Type 6 - The Loyalist.

Chapter 8: Type 6 - The Loyalist

Those in the Type Six group are also referred to as The Loyalists as it is stated in the late Riso's book, *Personality Types: Using the Enneagram for Self-Discovery*. Those who have this personality type indicated on the Enneagram model are extremely insecure, paranoid, anxious, nervous, and are very distrusting. They are always worried about what could possibly go wrong and have a hard time believing that anything actually can turn out just fine.

Sixes do not at all trust easily and have a strong sense of suspicion with no matter who is approaching them, and don't trust that any situation will have a good outcome. However, because of this constant state of worrying, Sixes are quite good at troubleshooting in general. But the anxiety and fear that they are living through as a result of their constant worrying, distrust, and suspicion engulfs them and prevents them from relaxing and enjoying anything and anyone.

The core reason that the Sixes are highly suspicious, anxious, and distrusting is that they are longing to look for something or someone they can trust. And those who have successfully proven themselves trustworthy to the Loyalist would have done something extraordinary since Sixes are so naturally distrusting.

Those who have earned the trust of any of the Sixes really would have had to move mountains to gain their trust. The unfortunate thing is that if the individual who had successfully gained the Loyalist's trust had done something to break it, then the Six would still continue to trust that individual. That even means that if the individual had left the Six's life as a result, the Six would still hang onto false hope that there is still something trustworthy about that individual - or even a situation if the situation had let the Six down after he or she had invested that energy to trust it. That is because it would shatter the Six if he or she came to terms with the fact that something or someone who he or she had struggled to trust actually did ruin it. Then that would be a sign that absolutely nothing or no one is trustworthy at all.

And because the Six is constantly looking for something or to someone to really believe in, they tend to become obsessed with something or someone who they think has the potential to give them what they need, which is their reason to trust them. This can easily get the Six into trouble as well. They could end up trusting the wrong person or thing, and they are more likely not going to be able to trust anyone who has their best interest at heart, or who are doing their job to help them.

For instance, the Loyalist would be difficult patients for doctors. That is because the Six would not at all trust what doctors are prescribing to them. Sixes would immediately think that they are being poisoned or that the doctor is giving them something that would purposely not help them which may be due to their personal gain.

Examples of the types that would fit into this group are those who believe in conspiracy theories such as the Earth being flat. This group has constantly expressed their distrust towards organizations such as NASA and believe that they are only gaining something by stating that the Earth is not flat. They have been accused by those that believe in this theory as manufacturing pictures of the Earth from space through CGI technology - which did not exist on this level in the 1960s when those images were first starting to come out.

Additionally, they will always believe that the Earth is flat even though there is no proof. This is a belief they will keep hanging onto because the nature of this personality type is to hold onto any idea that they believe must be true even though evidence everywhere has pointed out that there is no truth to this theory. The Sixes would dismiss those who have proof that their belief is false and accused them of saying those things for their own personal gain - even though that is the furthest from the truth. Remember, this group is called The Loyalist group for a reason. They don't trust easily and are yearning to believe in something and are yearning to trust something which means they will easily fall for the wrong thing or person!

The Loyalist group as children would have had severe separation anxiety since infancy, which is common for all babies regardless of how they end up turning out personality wise. However, the separation anxiety from their caregivers would last for a much longer time than it would for a child that is of another personality type. This type of separation anxiety would have caused them problems when they had entered school as well.

Eventually, they would have grown out of the infantile separation anxiety but would have still been quite anxious when it came to those who they believed were trustworthy leaving their side. And they would have a hard time making friends, for this reason, however, if a peer had proven to be trustworthy to them, then their trust would have been earned, or won.

If the Six did successfully make a friend during any stage of life whether it was during childhood or adulthood, then he or she would become anxious if their friend did not text them or call them at a certain time. And the Six would as a result always be the type to hover around their trusted friend because of the fact that they have to make sure that they really are trustworthy. Again, after all, the Six really did put a lot of their suspicions aside to be open to trusting that individual so that means the individual cannot let them down at all. And as it was mentioned before, the Six would still continue trusting the individual if he or she had let the Loyalist down due to hope and not wanting to face that that individual did let the Six down.

Sixes do have a hard time getting around in life because of their strong distrusting and anxious nature. This means their work and personal lives would be negatively affected as well. In the next section of this chapter, how Sixes are affected in the workplace will be covered in addition to the list of jobs that are ideal for this personality type.

Sixes In The Workplace

Sixes would have a difficult time at work as they would in all aspects of their lives. They would be the type to stay in a less than desirable job because they would fear to look for something better since there is always a catch of some sort. And for the Six to get the job that he or she is presently at, the employer would have had to gain their trust somehow. And even if the company that the Six is working for was decent at first, it does not mean it would stay that way. And even though the co-workers of the Six would have been looking for other jobs because of finding better opportunities, the Six would stay regardless.

The Six may know deep down that there may be something better out there. However, the suspicion of any other employer not being honest or the worry of coming into a problem at any new job would be greater than his or her willingness to look for a better opportunity. And the Six would have a very difficult time if he or she was laid off or fired because once again, false hope would be clenched onto by the Six. That would mean that the Six would keep hoping that the old employer would take him or her back, and even though that seldom happens, the Six would be unemployed for a long time.

The only thing that would motivate the Six looking for another job again is when the threat of eviction is very real because the Six would see that there is little money in the bank since it is not coming from anywhere else. This means the Six would think of looking for another job as biting the bullet and preparing him or herself from being let down by the future employer unless the employer actually proves themselves to be trustworthy. In that case, the Six will be comfortable at the job and will stay there as long as possible no matter how the working environment turns out.

If you had guessed that the Six would be a perfect fit for the predictable 9 to 5 office type of job, you are correct. That is the working environment that the Six feels the safest and the least threatened. Other job roles that the Sixes would be good for are:

- Writing

- Teaching preschool or elementary school children since they are not a threat

- Any type of job that involves animals since they are also not a threat

- Any type of job that involves activism since something positive can be created out of anything that causes frequent worrying

The worst type of jobs for the Sixes are:

- Financial planning

- Investing

- Law

- Any involvement with the food or hospitality and tourism industry

- Any type of job that involves risk-taking of any kind

And, the Sixes would have a hard time with personal relationships as this would have been quite easy to figure out. More of that will be covered in the next and final section of this chapter.

Sixes In Relationships

Based on the personality type of the Six, one would wonder if they would ever be in a position to get married or to end up in a serious relationship - or to even have friends at all. However, the answer to that question is, yes, for some Sixes they would end up having some friends and would end up getting married. Again, if the individual who has proven themselves to be trustworthy to the Six, then the Loyalist would be receptive.

However, the divorce rate for Sixes is low. That is because once they have earned trust, then it is very hard for the trust to go away even if some actions that their partners do causes them to be anxious such as not texting them in a timely manner. Unfortunately, there are many cases where the Sixes end up in abusive relationships because of the fear of leaving no matter how bad the situation is. Anything extreme would have to happen in a relationship for the Six to have a desire to leave.

And in cases where the Six ends up leaving an especially bad relationship, he or she would likely remain single for life due to the fact that if one partner had really broken their trust, then any subsequent partners would do the same. Unfortunately, as well, Sixes as parents would not encourage their kids to take risks at all and may unintentionally put fear into them about not trusting others so easily. They would also tell their kids to never get their hopes up for anything, which can be good advice from a realistic standpoint since things in life rarely do turn out as planned.

Though, when a Loyalist parent tells his or her children to never get their hopes up, they are not referring to staying realistic about any situation. They are literally saying that they are guaranteed to be disappointed by everything in life and that there are very few things in life to trust. This becomes a complicated issue especially when the children are naturally risk-takers which the Six would have a very difficult time accepting.

It is safe to say that the Six only will stick to his or her comfort zone and will pass that way of thinking and believing onto their children - because it is safe, and like any other parent with good intentions, they want their kids to be safe as well. That sums up the Six personality type. In the next chapter, Type 7 or the Enthusiast will be covered.

Chapter 9: Type 7 - The Enthusiast

Have you come across individuals who are always excited about what is just around the corner? If so, are these people always looking forward to the next best thing to experience and are not acknowledging what is happening in the now? Or does this description apply to you? Then if you answered yes to any of that, then there is a personality type that matches this characteristic as well on the Enneagram model. This type is the Type Seven group or Enthusiasts.

As it said in the late Riso's book, Personality Types: Using the Enneagram for Self-Discovery, Sevens are always looking forward to the future and are really the ones who are making the most of their lives, sometimes to excess. Sevens are always very optimistic and do not accept any type of negativity at all in life, which includes failure. They have a need to live in constant excitement, and really do forget to stop and smell the roses.

This group is always living in the future, and this means that they will be constantly planning exciting trips or outings. That means after they take one trip, then they will be looking forward to taking the next, and so on. And once their excitement over those trips ends, then they will find something else to look forward to. Perhaps they will want to seek some type of adventure that they have never experienced, or they will go towards great lengths to meet a celebrity without taking in account that they will have to get through plenty of security to get to them.

Here is an example of what goes on with a Seven. He or she plans a trip to Africa to go on a safari which is an exciting opportunity that most people do not experience. However, once that trip is over, and even after gaining the experience of seeing a pride of lions closeup and personal, the Seven would forget that he or she had that experience and would then plan another trip to somewhere else such as India to see the Taj Mahal. And after that trip is over, then the same thing would happen again because this group is never appreciating what they had experienced and are always looking forward to the next best thing over and over again.

Even during the trip planning, the Seven would all of a sudden have an urge to go bungee jumping or skydiving or do something that the average individual would be apprehensive of doing. Part of their plans as well for the future is wanting to visit any celebrity by not even thinking about the fact that this type of thing is not at all easy to do - especially if you are just a random person that does not have any type of personal or business ties to the celebrity either. The Seven would be told this fact and would be warned that they would not be able to get through the tight security that is keeping the celebrity protected. The Seven's response would be to that "Who cares! They will let me in because this is part of my future plan and nothing will stop it from happening". Where is the logic to that? There is not any as that is unrealistic optimism which is what the Sevens are all about.

As you can imagine, they are highly energetic, extroverted, and are incredibly talented when it comes to multitasking as they can managing doing five jobs at once. In fact, they have an extreme spirit that is quite entrepreneurial as they can be highly successful business owners and are excellent networkers as well. They can be quite charming which is what attracts them to others.

However, it is a known fact that no one can stay so high for that long without crashing down, even the Seven and this is what gets them into trouble. The Sevens do anything they can possible to prevent themselves from experiencing a crash. And unfortunately, when they are faced with disappointments, they refuse to accept any of it. They are terrified of being in any kind of negative frame of mind and are the last group to be introspective. They will do anything they can to hang into any type of high as they will always magnify and even brag about their strengths and not acknowledge in any way at all that they have weaknesses.

Sevens do come off as narcissistic, and they can easily be prone to addictions for the sake of having that high feeling all the time. They can be addicted to shopping, gambling, food, alcohol, drugs or anything else that is clearly unhealthy. And the Sevens may be mistaken for the Three types. However, the main difference is that Threes have more of a one-track mind, unlike the Sevens.

The Sevens can also be mistaken for Fours when they are in their manic states which is often. However, the big difference with this is that Fours display that characteristic when they are embracing their pain which is behind them expressing themselves the way they do, and Sevens behave this way to escape from pain of any kind.

These traits would have been seen in early childhood. Kids that have the Seven personalities would appear to be spoiled because they would always beg their parents for a new toy and many times, they would successfully manipulate their parents into buying them the new toy they wanted. And that meant these children would quickly become bored with playing with the toys that their parents bought them and would always ask for new ones. For the ones whose parents refused would always have meltdowns over it. And they may have given up asking for new toys, but their adventure and pleasure-seeking personality would still show.

These are the kids that other parents fear that their kids would become involved with due to the fact that the young Seven would constantly get into trouble due to them always seeking new adventures and new thrills- which would, unfortunately, involve their peers since they are naturally extroverted. Sevens would be the types to experiment with drugs and alcohol at a young age, as well as getting into other forms of trouble. The average Enthusiast likely has been sent to the school's principal's office over and over again as well whereas the principals, the parents of the child, and the teachers would be stunned that the child would not learn his or her lesson after being in trouble so often.

That is because the Seven does not consider consequences and is just concerned about looking forward to the next adventure even if that means having to be in trouble and grounded over and over again. Seven children would be the type to be part of the popular crowd, and they would be the type of bully others for, unfortunately, the thrill, not considering how the victim would be affected at all. Sevens can be quite self-absorbed, and in order for them to be successful in the workplace, they would be the ones to seek jobs and go into fields that would make many people of different personality types uncomfortable.

Sevens In The Workplace

It is not hard to imagine that the Seven would take on career roles that would scare those with other personality types and the Seven would not at all do well in any type of routine 9 to 5 office type of job. They hate routine because routine lacks adventure and that is the Seven's worst nightmare.

They also know at the same time that they need to work in order to make money so they can live, but they will be very picky about the types of jobs they would have. Many of them would not want to take on a role that is looked down by others as well due to the fact that it could easily blemish their self-image. That being said, you will never see a Seven working in a factory, or stocking shelves in warehouses. There will be more about the types of jobs that clearly do not work for the Enthusiast soon. However, right now, the types of jobs that the Sevens are more suitable for are:

- Bartending

- Bar or nightclub owner

- Writing in the travel, beauty, or fashion

niche

- Most job roles that involve travel or that are in the travel niche

- DJ

- Acting

- Photography that involves plenty of traveling

- Music publicist

- Small business owner

- Life coach

- Fitness instructor

- Working with celebrities even if that means taking a job that they would not normally take

The jobs that the Sevens would not be at all the best fit for other than the ones previously mentioned are:

- Medicine

- Law

- Customer service

- Accountant

- Clerical work of any sort unless a celebrity was involved

- Any job that involves routine

This is why it is rare to see Enthusiast co-workers unless you are also in bartending as the Seven would be, which would be the least exciting job that they would accept. And they would do so out of necessity as well. The Seven would not even attempt working in a setting that involves having to sit in cubicles next to other co-workers. This is also indicative of the fact that even though Sevens can be fun to be around, they many times do not last being in long-lasting relationships which will be covered in the next and last section of this chapter.

Sevens In Relationships

Sevens are naturally charismatic at first as they have an easy time making friends with those who are open to seeking adventure. The only time that Sevens repel others, in general, is when they start becoming condescending by bragging about their virtues, so they don't allow their faults to show. In other words, their narcissistic ways can be a huge repellant.

However, the problem with the Seven when it comes to personal relationships is that they seldom last due to the fact that the Seven would easily become bored with the partner and could not be tied down due to their nature. Unfortunately, this is the group that is the most prone to adultery due to being bored with their partner and seeking excitement from other places and sources. Some of them with more honest tendencies would not cheat and just file for divorce instead which is easier for the partner to handle due to the fact that no deception was involved.

The fact of the matter is that the only time when the Seven would stay in a committed relationship would be if he or she was in a serious relationship with someone else who was just like them, and constantly was looking for adventure and pleasure. In fact, some couples who are avid travelers who may have stayed together for a long time may likely both be Sevens as they would channel their adventure in a healthier manner.

The majority would not stick around with the partner for a long time, and that would even mean them taking off even if kids were involved. Sevens as parents may be either absent in order to indulge their need for consistent pleasure or would be the type to keep taking their kids out of school to go on trips and would not be concerned about committing truancy.

The likelihood that more often than not, Sevens do not get married because they fear being tied down and would go through great lengths to prevent that. Some are seen as commitment-phobic which they are, but it has nothing to do with them having bad past experiences with relationships. It all boils down to them taking off on a relationship that is becoming serious due to the fact that the Seven knows that if a marriage happened, then the fun would end, and rules would have to take its place.

That covers the Enthusiast personality type on the Enneagram model. The next personality type that will be covered in the next chapter is the Type 8 - The Challenger.

Chapter 10: Type 8 - The Challenger

The Type 8 group are those who are all about control, and any Eight is also called The Challenger. As it is stated in the late Riso's book, *Personality Types: Using the Enneagram for Self-Discovery*, Eights are literally all about control which has absolutely nothing to do with them being on any type of power trip for petty reasons.

Just like the Sevens, the Eights are extremely assertive, are always hungry for freedom, will not stand to be controlled in any way or form, and will bypass authority of any kind to attain it, and are incredibly energetic as well. However, the big difference between the Sevens and the Eights is that the Sevens are multi-focused as they are always looking for the next best thing. The Eights are power focused on one thing which they will go towards great lengths to attain what they are focused on, and they are also quite practical which the Sevens are not.

Eights not only refuse to be controlled by others but will not allow outside circumstances to have any kind of control over them. They absolutely do not accept the truth that there are situations in life that are out of one's hands. The Eights will do anything they can to manipulate anything just to have control over it which even includes doing something about any type of situation that normally would be out of one's hands.

However, this trait is not necessarily a negative thing if it is kept in control which would only be by the Eight agreeing to keep the trait in control for reasons of his or her own. For instance, if the Eight realized that he or she had extra weight to lose and had a desire to lose it, nothing would stop the Eight from attaining that goal because of the fact that they are in control of their health and their bodies.

Though, an Eight making the decision to lose weight would not be a common situation unless he or she had a reason of his or her own to make that change that had nothing to do with any type of the external influence. The Eight would never stand for that. That is because their appetites are hearty; they will indulge without feeling guilty or shameful in any way at all. Their instincts are also quite bold. And perhaps they need extra energy in order to keep going after their lofty goals which may be why their appetites are quite strong.

Based on what was written so far about the Eight personality type of the Enneagram model, you would think they would lack any type of vulnerability. However, just like the other personality types, Eights can be just as vulnerable and sentimental as the others. They also know this deep down, and they refuse to allow anyone to see it. They will never allow anyone to peg them as weak as they also refuse to lower their defenses in any situation. And, just like the Sixes, Eights do not trust easily either.

However, once the Eight do trust, then they can

make a friend for life, and even become their fiercest protector if necessary. They can be loyal as well. Though, if the Eight is ever betrayed by anyone who he or she trusted, then the Challenger could become violent towards the offender. That is the difference between how the Sixes and the Eights handle being betrayed after being let down by the one who they had lowered their guards to trust.

The Sixes fantasize about a part of the offender being trustworthy again whereas the Eights will retaliate without any hesitation and can be emotionally or physically violent. They may be known as well for their gaslighting tactics.

This trait would have been easily detected in early childhood. The child may have been a quick developer as he or she would have had the instinct at an early age to become the master. It is not unusual for Type Eight toddlers to potty train quickly, but it would have been in their own terms. Not all Type Eight children would have wanted to master that skill so quickly just to be in control.

However, as the type Eight child matured and aged, they would have been the types to be high achievers and at the same time, popular but also would have not hesitated to bully those who they perceived as weak. They would have been the first ones to pick on peers who would have fit as Fours because of the fact that their eccentricities made them appear weak and would have caused them to be targeted.

Eights have a low tolerance for those who are perceived as weak as they have no compassion for them at all. Even though the Eights have been high achievers, they would have clashed with teachers due to power struggles. And many Eight boys in high school would have been the typical stereotypical jocks you would see. The girls would be the stereotypical cheerleaders who had the perfect body and would shame other girls who did not have a perfect figure as they did.

The Challengers would have been quite rebellious

at home with their parents all due to once again, reasons that had to do with control. They would be the ones to never come home at their curfew hour because if they did, that would have meant they would have had to abide by their parents' rules which they would never have done. They would also find a way out of a situation that involved punishment by their parents as well. And Eights would have left home early so they could be independent and would have found a way to make it on their own at even a young age.

And as you can imagine, the Eights would not do well in common workplace settings, and more detail about the Eights in the workplace will be covered in the next section of this chapter.

Eights In The Workplace

Eights can find independence at a young age and can find a way to be financially independent. They are willing to get the more menial type of jobs when they are kids, and just starting out on their own. As much as the Eight needs to have control over anything and everyone, they are also practical which was previously mentioned. They realize that they will need to start from the bottom in order to go to the top, unlike the Seven who believes they can go at the top immediately.

And, not all Eights end up going to college. Many are actually high school dropouts as well as runaways because of clashing with authority, and they make out on their own. They will only take courses for the sake of learning and improving themselves so they can be financially independent so no one can ever have control over them at all.

That also means that once Eights are more established, then the types of career roles that are ideal for them are:

- The manager or the director of sales

- Real estate agent or developer due to their go-getting and aggressive personality

- Politician

- Marketing or advertising executive

- The head of publicity

- Freelance strategist

- Internet marketer

- Motivational speaker

- The CEO of anything

And the worst possible jobs for the Eights are:

- The average clerical 9 to 5 office job unless they are starting from the bottom

- Retail work

- Any type of job that is all about having a routine and does not have growth potential

The Eights will only start out at entry level jobs as long as there is a potential to be promoted. That also means that the high school dropouts looking for work will also have that in mind. They will take a routine-based entry-level job as long as there is a chance that they can be promoted. They will not like having to do the monotonous work and will hate even more that they will have a boss, but their practical nature causes them to give into it since they know they cannot climb to the top without starting at the bottom.

Either way, however, the Eight will find a way to be financially independent because their drive is unstoppable. And, they are frequently the multi-millionaire internet marketers who tell their stories about how they had an unstoppable drive since childhood and how they dropped out of school. They will talk about the challenges they endured and successfully conquered along the way which is how they made it to where they are currently standing.

The Eights who have it in them to be empathetic towards others, which they all have a sentimental side that they hide unless they are reassured that their softer side will not be watered down by their need to be in control. The Challengers who fit this description are those who you do see as strong and successful motivational speakers who want to help others find it within themselves to be in control of their lives - so as long as it does not threaten their own.

They do that by telling others to inspire their stories, and even though the Eights are naturally the type to be in control, the ones who are motivational speakers teach others how to find it within themselves to be in control of their own lives.

This states right there that in some cases, Eights do relate to others, but will only agree to help others who do not pose a threat to them. That means they will only be around others willingly who they know will never be in control of them. Eights don't trust easily which was mentioned, so they still keep others at arm's length even when it comes to those who they want to inspire.

More about Eights and relationships will be covered in the next and last section of this chapter.

Eights In Relationships

Many Eights do end up alone because of the fact that they do not trust easily and are afraid to let their guard down when it comes to being intimate in any way. They fear that if they end up in relationships with others, then they will be controlled by them or the circumstances that they can bring into the relationship. This is why many Eights don't settle down and have kids either.

That is because kids control parents and the average Eight will not want to ever be in a situation that will cause them to be controlled in any way at all. However, for the Eights that do get married and have kids, they would have had to have been convinced in a strong way to get into a serious relationship at all, to begin with. Sometimes their hearts are won by those who the Eights find to be irresistible and, in those cases, as long as those who they are in a relationship with are always trustworthy, the Eights will protect them in a fierce way.

For the Eights that are open to becoming parents, they would be both fiercely protective as well as controlling. They will never allow their kids to go against their rules, but at the same time, they would go great lengths to keep their kids safe.

However, the majority of Eights do not settle down and get married because of their intense trust issues as well as their refusal to allow themselves to be controlled in any way at all. The common goal of the Eight is to be as independent as possible so they can never give any of their monetary wealth to anyone and so they can be in complete control of themselves and their situations.

In the next chapter, the last personality type of the Enneagram model will be covered. That is the Type 9 which is The Peacemaker.

Chapter 11: Type 9 - The Peacemaker

After reading the first eight personality types, you would have noticed a pattern. And the pattern would be that each of the first eight types has plenty of strong negative and self-serving traits. They are all different, and some are more extreme than others, but each and every personality type from the Enneagram model shows the negative traits are due to something they are afraid of that is in the deepest part of their core. However, the Type Nine which is the last personality type on the Enneagram model is different somewhat.

Those who are part of this type are also referred to as The Peacemakers as it is mentioned often in the late Riso's book, *Personality Types: Using the Enneagram for Self-Discovery*. And, Nines do have their challenges as well, but their overall personality is based on genuinely what they are called, which is the peace-making type.

Nines really do have the best intentions at heart and want to make sure everyone is happy, are healthy, and have their needs met. They are easy-going, trusting, faithful, charismatic and likable, reliable, and tolerant people and these traits that they have are genuine. However, Nines are far from perfect because they absolutely cannot stand conflict and will avoid any potential for it at all costs.

With that said, many Nines are introverted and do withdraw from others. However, this is not the case with all Nines. Some of them are sociable, and some of them are sociable on their own terms. Most of them do need time alone to recharge as being around too many people can be draining to them for prolonged periods of time. This may sound contradictory since they do feel connected to others, but at the same time, they don't want to be around people for too many hours in a day. This may mean they feel connected to others on a more spiritual approach. They also feel connected to the world in general on a spiritual level.

Nines also are the types to believe that things work out, even if it means that they end up working out in a different way that they had imagined. For instance, the Nine may be writing a book and has the belief that a publisher will pick up the book and accept it. However, the Nine faces a different reality and none of the publishers that he or she pitches to accept the book. However, the Nine decides to self-publish the book and ends up finding an opportunity that is relevant to the subject matter through a buyer of the book that was impressed that contacted the Peacemaker to offer an exciting opportunity.

This way, the Nine would have not had the book accepted by the publishers that he or she had pitched to but had decided to self-publish the book and attract a buyer who loved it. And the buyer loved it to the point that he or she offered the Nine an excellent opportunity that was related to the book. And things did end up working out in the end, but not in the way the

Nine had imagined. And, he or she would have been at peace with it as well.

However, there are some negative traits that the Nines possess that are less serious than the other personality types. Firstly, Nines are resistant to change and prefer to keep things the way they are. But if they are forced to change in any way which at one way or another they are since life is all about evolving and changing, they do adapt much better than they give themselves credit for.

The Nines also are incredibly hard on themselves and will berate themselves for not doing something right or for hurting someone or something when they would not have been responsible for it. They also are too kind to the point that they can be easily taken advantage and taken for granted by those who prey on them. However, they still get angry. If they are angered, they will not react right away. They are the types to allow the anger to build up until they end up exploding and end up saying words that they would regret after the fact.

Some Nines will not explode if they are angry and will become passive-aggressive by dishing out the silent treatment or they can be deceptive on purpose to spite someone who did them wrong. And Nines can be grudge-holders as well which may be surprising to learn since this type would be believed to be the forgiving type.

Not all Nines are grudge-holders, as the ones who are slowly angered to the point of exploding will be likely to let it go and blow over after getting those emotions out. The Nines that are the ones that are the most likely to be grudge-holders are those who are the types to express their anger through passive-aggression.

All of the traits from the Nines would have been noticeable since early childhood. Nines as toddlers would have been like any other toddler to throw tantrums when they don't get their way because that is how they learn about themselves or their needs. However, Nines as children will be seen as affectionate, and empathetic at a young age.

As they grow and mature, and reach the age where they start attending school, they will show this kindness to their peers, and be the type to please their teachers as well. However, as much as you would think they would stand up for the underdog or if they see a child being bullied, they would not only because they are terrified of conflict. They may, however, befriend the bully victim and spend time with him or with her privately, somewhere in the school yard away from the other kids since they need their space.

However, if the Nine as a child was seen with the victim, that would mean that the Nine would easily become a victim of bullying as well. And the Nine would run away from the bully to avoid conflict at all costs.

This also means that the Nine child would obey the parents and always follow their rules, and they would have been terrified to get into trouble. They would carry this trait throughout their personal and professional lives as well.

In the next section, Nines in the workplace will be covered.

Nines In The Workplace

Many types of jobs and career roles are a good fit for the average Nine type. The Nine would do just fine working in a typical office 9 to 5 working environment and would even be the type to pass on any promotion to others if he or she felt that the other would have been more deserving. This is how the Nines can do themselves a disservice. This type of working environment would be ideal as well because of the fact that the average Nine does not like change in any way at all and needs to be in his or her comfort zone. That is another reason that the Nine would be likely to pass up a promotion due to the fact that promotion means that they would have to meet higher expectations such as having to work overtime and having to fulfill other duties that the Nine would not be comfortable with.

The Nine would just want to keep things as they

are. Go to work, then leave at 5 pm (or whatever hour it would be based on the hours he or she is working), and go home, have dinner, walk the dog, and do the nightly duties whether that involves their family or not. They would be completely content with doing this for the rest of their working years.

Sometimes, the Nine would want to make a change of some sort, but it would have to be on their own terms as they cannot handle the idea of being thrown into it. However, they do adapt better than they believe they can as it was previously mentioned. There have been many times that Nines have been fired or laid off, and they had been able to settle themselves into new jobs, especially if the jobs that they had found were similar to the ones they had previously.

Other than the predictable office 9 to 5 office job, the best jobs or career options for the Nines would be:

- Therapist

- Creative writer

- Writer in softer niches

- Creativity coach

- Human resources manager

- Social worker

- Mediator

- Teacher

- Editor

- Youth group leader

- Activist

- Any type of work with animals

- Any type of work with the disabled

The worst possible career roles or jobs for the Nines would be:

- A CEO of any company unless they have a reason to be self-employed

- Lawyer

- Banking

- Investment banking

- Financial advisor

- Anything that involves risk or being antagonizing in any way or form.

None of this would at all be surprised to learn that the Nines would be a good fit for some jobs or careers, and a poor fit for some others as it the same would apply for all personality types.

This also means that the Nines present themselves in such a way when it comes to their personal relationships which will be covered in the last section of this chapter.

Nines In Relationships

Based on what you have learned about the Nine type personality, it would not be surprising to learn that the Peacemakers make incredibly loyal partners. They would have been the types to always put the needs of others ahead of themselves. Sadly, many of them would have also been taken advantage of and taken for granted as their kindness would have been easily misused.

Nines would be the ones to be hurt easily in relationships such as being lied to or even being cheated on as well. However, the problem is that the Nines would become angry and hurt over that kind of deception. However, the Nine would also do anything to avoid conflict and end up causing the anger over being deceived into boiling up which means an explosion would end up happening. Or, the Nine would become passive-aggressive and deceive the partner as a result or do something else in a passive-aggressive way.

This also means that the Nine would have a relationship that lacks conflicts which is also not healthy, as the Nine would be building up anger and resentments for not getting his or her needs met and staying quiet about it. This means the partner would have no idea that the Nine would be upset regardless of whether the partner doing anything to intentionally upset or hurt the Nine. Communication is lacking in marriages and relationships with the Nine type which would present challenges.

The same would apply to their friendships, and the same would apply to their parenting tactics. Nines would make excellent parents because they would make sure their kids' needs are met; however, they would not be the ones to discipline them effectively because that would involve conflict otherwise. They would not want to be the cause for their kids to throw a tantrum, and unfortunately, that means their kids could become unruly due to not having enough discipline.

There needs to be balance in regard to parenting roles in that case to offset that situation.

This completes the 9 personalities of the Enneagram model, and that is not what completes the model either. There are more facets to the Enneagram as the next chapter will cover one of the other facets, which are the wings.

Chapter 12: The Enneagram Wings

There is a lot more to the Enneagram than the 9 personality types that were covered over the last 9 chapters. The personalities are just one aspect of the model, and chances are after you had read about the personality types, you had wondered if anyone really has personalities that are so extreme which were described in each of the chapters. The odds of that being the case are low because even though the personality types are what people's cores are like, they are usually watered down or influenced by other personality types.

The reasons that the personality types are colored or are influenced are because part of the Enneagram model consists of wings, which are responsible for altering the personality types as it is referenced in the late Riso's book, *Personality Types: Using the Enneagram for Self-Discovery*.

If you remember back earlier in the eBook that the personality types were compared to having a plain flavored vanilla ice cream, that in itself seems bare. The same goes for personality types. However, what you need to change it up and to flavor, it is to add toppings which could be fudge sauce, caramel sauce, or sprinkles, or nuts, whatever you choose, that is what makes the ice cream sundae more complete. The ice cream or sundae toppings are what the wings of the Enneagram model represent. The spice that is added to the core in order to make the individual more complete.

In other words, the wings are the neighboring personality types that are right next to the core type on the Enneagram model. These wings do influence your core, but they do not alter your core type just like the sundae toppings do not change the fact that the type of ice cream that they are laid over is the vanilla ice cream.

Here is a better analogy to make this clearer. Our core type is our personality type. That represents the vanilla ice cream, but if you put fudge sauce over it, then that represents the influence of one neighboring wing type. And if you put sprinkles on it, then that represents the other neighboring wing's influence on the other side.

However, in some cases, both wings are highly influential, and in other cases, one wing is more influential than the other, and that all depends on the circumstance that the individual is in. These wings are helpful and can be resourceful, and they are also there to help balance the individual as well.

Think back again to the airplane analogy. An airplane needs its wings in order to stay balanced in the air. The core by itself will not be able to do that job. The wings help keep the individual balanced as the core type by itself would not be able to maintain that type of balance at all.

The purpose of the wings is to help bring a new perspective to an individual when they are faced in any type of challenging or any type of situation. The wings also are beneficial when it comes to emotions and behavior. Let's take a look at some examples of how the wings can be beneficial to each of the 9 personalities on the Enneagram model in the next section as it will start from Type 1 to Type 4.

Type One To Type Four And Their Wings

In this section, you will learn about the first 4 types of personalities and how their types are altered by their wings when necessary:

Type 1 - The Perfectionist - The perfectionist only wants perfection and cannot stand anything that is less than perfect. The main fear that the One has is that he or she is afraid of being corrupt in any way and wants to be balanced and have integrity. The wings will help create more balance for the Ones. The Type One with a Nine wing would have influences from the Nine personality type and would provide them with a calmer approach. They still have their strong expectations, but they will be able to allow things to unfold when they rely on the Nine wing.

The Type One with a Two wing will be more of an advocate. They want perfection, and they want to help make a situation better. If a Type One goes into a homeless shelter and sees that there is abuse going on, and wants to improve things for the situation, then the One will lean on to the Two wing to advocate for the safety and better treatment of the individuals.

Type 2 - The Helper - The helper wants to please others and be there for others but has a strong possessive side. However, if Type Two relies on the One wing, then that shapes the individual for being more of a servant to others. That does not literally mean they will be maids or butlers. However, they will be the ones to deliver messages to others to make sure it is delivered properly.

Type Two with a Three wing will be the type to host events or to teach others what they have learned that can be helpful. They still want to be appreciated, and that is why those with this personality type who learn on Wing Three will be the ones to hold events or to go and teach in settings that they know that they will get their kudos for putting themselves out there.

Type 3 - The Performer - The performer is naturally charming and is only concerned about being ambitious for the sake of being the best at what they do. And they want to beat their competition as well. And, in order for them to win others over, even more, they will rely on their Two Wing in order to help others which means that they will gain what they need.

This sounds like they are strictly taking advantage of people in order for them to win, but when they rely on their Two Wing, they will genuinely help someone who is in need, but they do need to get something back from it. When the Three leans on the Four Wing, they tap into their unique side and turn it into something professional. Type Threes that are entrepreneurs have to lean towards the Four Wing in order to differentiate themselves from the competition.

Type 4 -The Romantic - This individualistic type is always looking for ways to seek out their identity because of how they fear that they have no real significance. They are quite melodramatic as well. However, the Fours that lean on their Three Wing can be unique yet have an approach to go after something which will give them confidence that they have a purpose to fulfill.

The Four that leans on the Five Wing will be more like a Bohemian, as they will realize that they are unique and will embrace it without having to make their mark. They will not throw their uniqueness in people's faces and will find a way to live comfortably with who they are on their own.

The next and final section of this chapter will focus on Type 5 to Type 9 personalities and its wings.

Type Five To Type Nine And Their Wings

In the late Riso's book, *Personality Types: Using the Enneagram for Self-Discovery* plenty of information about the personality types and their wings on the Enneagram model are covered. In the previous section, the brief descriptions of the Type One to Type Four personalities and their wings were covered. In this section, the Type Five to Type Nine personality types and their wings will be focused on before going into the next chapter which is going to be about the Enneagram centers.

However, before that is covered, let's finish this chapter by covering the wings for the Type Five to Type Nine personality types on the Enneagram model.

Type 5 - The Investigator - As you know that the Fives are quite secluded, and secretive, and they are the observers, and they spend their time gathering up information. They are not the type to make friends easily unless they find someone who they relate to and can become friends for life. In fact, their main fear is that they may end up useless and incapable. And their greatest yearning is that they are competent.

However, when the Investigator leans on the Four Wing, they become more of an iconoclastic type. They are the types that are ready to break traditions and are extremely bold thinkers. They are not afraid to rebel, and that is how they can work through their insecurities if necessary. For instance, the Five that is appalled by how a cult is brainwashing a group of people because the Five has already done research of their own to see how damaging they are can easily lean on the Four Wing in order to make a bold move by exposing the type of damage the cult has caused with proof. That will most definitely make people wake up, especially the ones who have been affected.

The Fives that learn on the other wing, which is the Six Wing end up becoming problem-solvers.

The Fives are distrusting like the Sixes are, however, the Sixes are the ones that yearn to find someone or something to trust which is the biggest challenge for the Six. If the Five comes across something or someone that they are attracted to, then they can learn towards their Six Wing in order to determine how trustworthy someone is, or whether getting involved in something they are interested in is worth it. They will evaluate whether the individual or situation deserves a chance through critical thinking.

Type 6 - The Loyalist - The Loyalist is always distrusting and yearns to find something or someone to trust. They want to be committed to something or to someone and need security. However, even though they are responsible and engaging, they are extremely anxiety-ridden and suspicious. They are terrified without having support or proper guidance, and their main desire is to have the support they need as well as the security as they do not like going out of their comfort zones.

The Type Six with a Five-Wing are the types to defend others if they know they are innocent in a situation or understand their situation as to why they did something that may be unpopular. For instance, if a worn-out parent had no choice but to put their disabled child into a group home and he or she received nothing but judgment and criticism for it, then the Loyalist leaning on the Five Wing would stand up and defend the parent. Even though the Loyalist would not understand on a personal level why the parent did what he or she needed to do, the Six would understand that the parent was burned out and could not help the child and would not hesitate to point that out to those who are judging the parent.

The Six leaning on a Seven Wing would be the type to leave their comfort zone a little and put their distrusting trait aside if they saw someone who was distraught. And, in this case, the Six would sit down next to the individual to listen to why he or she is quite upset just to give that person an ear. The Sixes are all about needing comfort and the Seven breaks the comfort zone, and in this case, the Seven Wing would help break that.

Type 7 - The Enthusiast - Sevens are adventure seekers and are naturally positive. They need to constantly have their needs fulfilled as to why they are always looking forward to the next best thing, and they are terrified of being deprived. The Sevens are not empathetic, but the Sixes are, and when the Sevens lean on their Six Wing, they want to make others happy who are having a rough time. That is why they are referred to as the entertainers, as they can easily cheer someone up who is having a bad day.

The Sevens are also not naturally practical or organized; however, their neighboring personality type the Eight is both powerful and practical. And when the Seven realizes that he or she has to be grounded to attain a goal, then this is when he or she leans on the Eight Wing and is just as powerful but is more realistic and organized about attaining a certain goal.

Type 8 - The Challenger - Type Eight is the bold, dominating, and confident type, and will never back down if a challenge is being faced. Those who have this personality type will not back down and are the ones who must always be in charge. Their biggest yearning is that they are always in charge no matter what, and that applies to life circumstances. They are deeply afraid of being controlled or harmed by others.

However, the Eights need to lean on their wings when it comes to certain situations. And the Eight has to realize at times that he or she cannot control life's circumstances and the only way that the Eight can find acceptance is by leaning on the Seven Wing. This causes the Eight to become innovative and creative by finding a solution to be in charge of an outside circumstance that cannot be changed.

For instance, if an Eight was on a ship that was about to sink, he or she would jump off and swim over to a foreign island where he or she would not know anything about which includes the language. The Eight would find a way to learn a language and find temporary work to stay there until he or she could find a way to get back home or to the destination where he or she was heading.

And, for the Eight that needed to be in a position to protect someone else's needs, then they would lean on the Nine Wing for not just being the protector but being empathetic towards the one who needed protection. The Eight would lean on the Nine Wing to be concerned about someone else's needs other than their own if there was a situation that came up. For instance, the Eight could find a homeless individual who had been bullied. This would trigger the empathetic side in the Eight, and the Eight would then fight off the bully to help the homeless individual, and then even go and buy them a meal. That would be the result of them leaning on the Nine Wing.

Type 9 - The Peacemaker - This personality type is naturally empathetic, loyal, receptive, agreeing, complacent, and easygoing. They only want to have peace of mind, and their biggest fear is experiencing a loss. The Nine needs to lean on the Eight or One Wings in order to be in better control of their situations as well as the situations of those who they care for because without either of these wings, they will not survive with this personality type alone.

Nines that lean on the Eight Wing are referred to as the advocates. They are naturally empathetic; however, in some situations they need to be in better control of themselves or of others that are close to them. If they are in a situation where they are not getting the medical help they need for an illness they suspect they have, then they would need to lean on the Eight Wing and become bold and become their own advocates in order to receive better medical care. Or if their children were struggling in school and the teachers were not concerned, then they would be an advocate for their children to make sure that they get the type of help or education they are entitled to get. In other words, when push comes to shove, the Nine will need to rely on the Eight Wing.

And, the Nine will need to rely on the One Wing in order to turn their dream into a reality. Nines by themselves are not grounded. However, they have the ability to be, and that is when they can lean on the One Wing. The One Wing will help gain the skills and knowledge to turn their dream into something that really comes to live instead of just staying as a fantasy.

For instance, if the Nine wanted to become an author and even become a best-seller, then the Nine would investigate what could be done to make that happen by leaning on their Perfectionist Wing.

And that concludes the Wings of the Personality Types Of The Enneagram. The examination of the Enneagram model is not finished as the next chapter will be covering the centers which are also covered in the late Riso's book, *Personality Types: Using the Enneagram for Self-Discovery*.

Chapter 13: Introduction To Centers

The onion of the Enneagram has been peeled a lot as you had already discovered it's 9 personality types, and then after learning about those, you had learned about how the personalities are tempered by their wings. And now, you are going to be learning about the centers in the Enneagram model. All of the information about the centers are derived from the late Riso's book, Personality Types: Using the Enneagram for Self-Discovery.

The 9 personality types of the Enneagram model are placed into the 3 groups which are called the centers. Each center represents the imbalances that are found in each of the personality type, which is where the negative traits of each one happens to lie. The 3 centers are the Instinctive center, the Feeling center, and the Thinking center. And each center contains the 3 personality types that share the strengths and weaknesses of that center.

Each type of personality is affected by the unconscious emotional response to not being in contact with the core in the centers. That is why the centers have negative themes. The themes of the centers are:

- **The Instinctive Center** as the One, the Nine, and the Eight personality types fall into this area, and this area represents rage and anger

- **The Feeling Center** as the Two, the Three, and the Four personality types also fall into this center, and this area represents shame

- **The Thinking Center** as the Five, the Six, the Seven personality types falls into this area as well, and this center represents fear.

After reading about the personality types more in detail, then it is not difficult to understand how these personality types could end up falling into the centers that best represent their traits. The first center that will be examined more is the Instinctive center, and the One, the Nine and the Eight personalities will be examined further as to how they are affected by the centers.

The Instinctive Center

The Instinctive center is represented by anger and rage, and it is easy to see how the Eights can be full of anger and rage but may be more difficult to understand how the Nines and the Ones are affected. Let's look further into each of the personalities that fall into this center more carefully.

The Eights affected by the Instinctive center - The Eights are all about needing to be in control, and the anger they have is instinctive, and it builds which is what strengthens their motivations. However, even with the positive side to the anger in this personality type which is put to good use. If they feel as if they are about to lose control, then rage sets in. Their rage setting in is the response to them feeling threatened by a person or a situation that could potentially have control over them.

This results in rage which causes them to easily express violence. The Eights respond to their anger in a physical way which includes them being physically violent as well as them raising their voices. Their natural, confident nature is what gives them permission to express anger in this manner. However, the Nines are fueled by anger as well as they express it differently based on their personality type.

The Nines affected by the Instinctive center - The Nines are in the same center as the Eights, and this may be difficult to believe since they are opposites personality wise. But they are equally effectively by anger and rage based on the fact that they lie in the Instinctive Center. However, whereas the Eights embrace their anger, the Nines do not as they deny it even though they are aware it is there.

The Nines shove it away as they are not in touch with this part of them in addition to their other instincts. Nines prefer to stick to their idealizations of the world. but if they are pushed, then that anger either comes bubbling up in an explosive manner or ends up affecting them by causing them to express their anger in a passive-aggressive way. The Nines avoid their anger, and the Ones also do not embrace and express their anger the same way as the Eights do, but in a different way.

The Ones affected by the Instinctive center - The Ones are all about perfection, and if they acknowledge their angry part, they feel as if they are less than perfect which is their ultimate nightmare. This is why the Ones do what they can do repress this side to them. They do not want to ever want to be seen as angry. However, as much as they want to deny the anger, they can't. The way they channel this instinctive anger is by directing towards their inner-critic and are also quite critical of others in a way that can sting.

The Eights express this anger in a violent and visible way, the Nines do to not acknowledge it, but it comes bubbling up through an explosive temper that is momentary or causes them to become passive-aggressive, and the Ones express this anger by being overly and unfairly critical of themselves and of others.

That concludes the way the Instinctive center effects personality types One, Nine, and Eight of the Enneagram model. The next center to examine is the feeling center.

The Feeling Center

The Feeling center is governed by the feeling of shame which affects personality types Two, Three, and Four. The first one to be examined is how the Twos are affected by this center.

The Twos affected by the Feeling center - The Twos are well aware of their feelings of shame and the way they suppress it is by focusing heavily on how they can be liked by others. And as long as they feel that they are appreciated, they can focus on the positive feelings they have while suppressing any feelings of shame that they may be having. And the way they want people to like them and appreciate them in a desperate way is by helping others, and this even means they would be putting their own wants and needs aside just to suppress their feelings of shame.

And, when they are threatened by someone who doesn't like them or if they do not feel appreciated, they are exposed to that shame, and this actually causes them to become angry. Their personality type is not in the Instinctive center, but shame also can bring up angry emotions which is why they are constantly feeling hysterical when they are not feeling appreciated for their efforts. The Threes also are doing what they can to suppress their feelings of shame in a different manner.

The Threes affected by the Feeling center - The Threes want to prove to themselves and to everyone else that they are winners in everything they do. They want to be the best at what is most important to them whether it is financial success or having the best-fit body. And they are constantly attempting to become the best in order to shove those uncomfortable feelings of shame which is why they are terrified of failure and feeling like they are adequate. Their extreme desire to be the best at what they do is so that they suppress their inner feelings of shame.

The positive attribute of this personality type is that this type is naturally driven even though it is for the wrong reasons. The Fours are governed by the Feeling center as well but in a much different way than the Twos and the Threes.

The Fours affected by the Feeling center - The Threes do what they can do avoid feelings of inadequacy whereas the Fours are most likely to succumb to those feelings of shame instead. However, what the Fours do in order to hide those feelings is that they show off their creativity, proudly show off their eccentricities, and make their mark about being unique as well.

Fours also are affected by feelings of shame by creating a fantasy life which causes them to escape from them having to deal with anything uncomfortable that life continuously throws at them. They do this to not only escape anything that can cause them hardships, but they do this by escaping anything that does not interest them in the least bit.

That concludes the personalities affected by the Feeling center. The last center that will be focused on is the Thinking center which effects the Five, the Six and the Seven personality types.

The Thinking Center

The Thinking center is governed by fear and the Five, the Six and the Sevens are the personalities that fall into this center, which is easily seen after learning about the nature of these personality types. The first one to be covered is how the Fives are affected.

The Fives affected by the Thinking center -

The one thing that the Fives fear the most is the external world. This is why they withdraw, are secretive and are observant, and learn what they can. They create their own inner worlds and will only allow those in it who they feel are not a threat in any way at all. Fives are seen as hermits because that is what they literally are in order to escape the outer world by keeping themselves within. They don't feel confident enough to join into the outer world, and this is based on their fear, which is why they keep to themselves.

The Sixes affected by the Thinking center - This personality type is affected by this center the most as they display plenty of anxiety over distrusting situations and people. And yet they have a strong desire to trust and have faith in others and in situations. Their fear is what prevents them from putting their distrusting and skeptical sides aside. They always find reasons to not trust someone or something even if there has been proof indicating that the individual or situation is completely Kosher.

And, Sixes will even doubt those who they have allowed them into their lives due to the fact that their fear is keeping them from being open and trusting in any way or form. They will also deal with their fear by being confrontational towards those who they do not trust which is driven by their anxiety over any situation that is causing them to be doubtful in the first place.

The Sevens affected by the Thinking center - The Fives fear the external world whereas the Sevens fear the internal world and their fear is the reason that the Sevens are constantly looking for excitement through external sources. This is the one personality type that will not be introspective in any way or form because they have to constantly look for excitement and adventure in order to escape the one thing they fear the most - and that is the inner world.

With that said, Sevens are not purposely shallow by them wanting to keep taking expensive trips and are obsessed with meeting celebrities, famous people, and people who they find to be worthy. The Sevens are not non-appreciative about the fact that they just went on an expensive trip and are looking forward to the next one each and every time. They are not purposely being thankless and taking their blessings for granted that most people would not have a chance to take even once in their lifetimes. The Sevens behave this way because they are absolutely terrified of being in their inner world and they are terrified of being trapped in it. They keep themselves engaged, busy, and occupied in many different activities at once just to escape their inner world.

That means the next time you think that someone who may be shallow for going on expensive trips all the time and not appearing to be thankful for their experiences may not be any of that at all. They may just be one of those Sevens that constantly need to escape due to the fact that they are driven by fear of being trapped. Their fear stops them from sitting down, breathing, and to smell the roses.

BONUS CHAPTER: Enneagram in Relationships

Using the Enneagram in Your Relationship

Love is a common subject for humans all over the world. We strive for it, can't get enough of it, sing about it, write about it, and shout about it from the rooftops. Love is good; love is great, actually. It makes us feel unstoppable, supported, and ready for anything. Two people that choose to be a team and commit to one another is a special thing, an amazing feeling, and something we all like to hold on to. Unfortunately, because we consider love to be so high on our list of needs, it can also be incredibly painful - especially when we lose it.

Ultimately, the Enneagram is a tool to help you reframe your perspective. It helps you see things about yourself and about others and brings you on a journey of self-discovery and self-improvement.

When we reframe the way we look at ourselves and others, breaking it down into our motivations and not just actions or simple personality test, we are able to change and improve what happens in our lives. Using the Enneagram to reframe your perspective to improve your relationship is one of its many effective uses.

While the Enneagram is not a substitute for marriage counseling or therapy in more dire situations, it is an effective way to understand yourself and your partner. Doing so improves your relationship and opens up the opportunity for you both to grow together. In order to do all of this, you have to be working on self and you will have to have open and honest conversations with your partner. You'll find yourself reading your partner more than usual and in more depth. Don't be put off if your partner is returning the attention and reading you too; it means they are paying attention just like you, which is a positive thing.

Why Use the Enneagram in Your Relationship?

What does the Enneagram have to offer to your relationship? As already discussed, using the Enneagram for yourself will improve your relationships as a result. It's also hard not to try to type people once you dive into this. When it comes down to it, you will notice things without people telling you now that your eyes are open to it. Although it's difficult to avoid doing, it's best to have your partner type themselves rather than attempting to type them on your own. Perhaps showing them what your type is will interest them enough to take the test and read about the types to figure out their own. Knowing your partner's type will most certainly offer a great advantage for being able to overcome hurdles and anticipate their needs. There are plenty of ways the Enneagram can provide help and value to your relationship, as outlined below.

1. **Compassion and empathy**- Understanding one another is an amazing ability for any relationship. However, this can be hard to do. Using you and your partner's type, you'll be better able to come to a level

of compassion and empathy for one another. This will allow for faster and more effective conflict resolution and even the avoidance of conflict altogether. When it comes down to it, one of the most important things in any relationship is respect. Respect and empathy go well together, though they aren't the same thing. You can always respect your partner, even when you do not necessarily understand them or get where they're coming from. It is respect that will help keep your relationship healthy and functioning. Respect will go a long way on its own, but if you add some genuine understanding and empathy along with it, your relationship can truly thrive. The Enneagram is an excellent tool in both cases.

2. Conflict resolution and avoidance- As mentioned above, the Enneagram as a whole can provide great insights into people, which aids in faster and more effective conflict resolution or avoidance. Being able to understand where your partner is coming from, what motivates them, and why something might upset them more than someone else is a unique perspective the Enneagram provides you with (it's up to you to use the knowledge you have gained). This can be as simple as knowing how much conflict upsets a type nine and what you can say or do to ease it for them. For example, if you're dealing with a type nine, instead of upsetting them further with more confrontation, you can change the tone of the conversation, which typically will reduce conflict with this type.

3. **It can make you more humble**- We all have faults and strengths, and the Enneagram helps us identify those in ourselves. It can be hard to see these traits in ourselves otherwise, and many relationships have rocky patches because of this. When you can see where your shortcomings are, you are better able to work on them, make up for them, and embrace them, which can be extremely beneficial for a relationship. It can allow some open and honest conversations to be had which can also create more trust and understanding in a relationship. Knowing where you may be falling a little short can also help you see where some of your partner's frustrations lie and vice versa. No one is perfect; it is through self-discovery that we learn and come to terms with this and, as a result, we improve.

4. **Highlight your strengths**- Just as everyone has areas they can work on, we also all have areas we

excel in. The Enneagram can help you see where your strengths are, just as they can your downfalls. You and your partner should be celebrating and using these strengths to your advantage. Celebrate each other and your wins, have fun, and connect during these positive moments.

5. **Communication**- Communication is key in any relationship. Without it, we're all just living in our own little world and guessing at everything. That sounds exhausting and not like something that anyone wants to really do. There are many benefits to opening up the lines of communication. Everything doesn't have to be positive, but discussing even the most mundane and simple things can bring people closer together. When people can communicate effectively, they're able to thrive and work together. Having open and honest discussions without judgement allows for the sharing of feelings, fears, and desires, not just on the surface, but at the core of each of us. These kinds of conversations have incredible benefits for any relationship.

Areas of Your Relationship in Which the Enneagram Can Help

There is nothing better than knowing that someone else in this world genuinely understands you. It can be the most exciting experience to find someone who just gets you. These are the types of relationships people strive for and the ones that people think can only appear magically through sheer luck. This is not the case, though. It is something that can be learned and practiced. You have the ability to come to a great understanding for your partner - even if you are complete opposites.

There is no one you want to understand more than your partner, and who does not want that back in return? It's never too late to get a deeper understanding of the person you love. Here are three ways the Enneagram can help you strengthen your understanding:

1. **Core fears-** The Enneagram offers insights into fears that surround a person. Often, many of our traits, motivations, and behaviors are based on the things we fear most. Knowing where your partner's fear comes from will help

you understand where much of their conflict may stem from. When you can understand this, you're better able to support and comfort them, avoid conflict, and deal with conflict in more effective ways. Conflict won't stop, because it is a normal part of the human experience; however, it can be handled and dealt with in a simpler way, and it can certainly happen less. The more someone feels understood and supported, the better they will be able to cope and get back on track to integration and happiness.

2. **Motivation-** The Enneagram offers insight into people's general motivations in life, such as what they do, what they pursue, and why they pursue certain things. Knowing this about your partner is an excellent place to start. Being aware of what drives, inspires, and motivates someone to do things can help you to be more attentive and supportive of that person, and it will allow you to dig deeper. We are not talking about superficial things, here (although in some cases, that may very well be the case), but rather the deeper core desires

we all have that are similar to the fears above.

3. **Emotions-** It can be hard for many people to feel vulnerable by sharing their emotions honestly, even within a loving relationship. The Enneagram can assist in figuring out what is driving any kind of moods or mood changes. It can show us when our partners are doing well and healthy and also when they are not doing so well. Knowing this allows you to put the proper precautions and support into place. Sometimes this is hard to see in ourselves, as we may know it's happening but perhaps not why. When partners can help us be on top of this, they can start pointing it out to us in a helpful way, which is a good spot to begin.

Spiritual Relationships with the Enneagram

The Enneagram has become very popular in certain religious and spiritual circles. There's something to be said for using the Enneagram in such cases - especially as it relates to your own relationships. The

Enneagram is a unique tool to develop self-awareness, and that fits well into a spiritual context

Because the Enneagram is rooted in ancient wisdom, it lends itself well to modern day spiritual people. Tools that already exist specifically for spirituality have concepts that are often difficult to grasp or their executions are too abstract.

Depending on your beliefs, the Enneagram can be used to deepen your connection with self, but it can also deepen your connection with a higher power. In this sense, it can be used to map out your spirituality or your religious motivations. Using the Enneagram to do this gives you a clearer picture of yourself and shines a light on your motives or your fears to uncover what drives you. Many beliefs out there strive for and encourage self-improvement and to be the best you can be.

In many households and relationships, spiritual beliefs are something that are fundamental to them. If this sounds like you and your relationship with spirituality, the Enneagram can also be used to strengthen the connection of your relationship to a higher power.

This is something you can do together as a couple, as well. You can introduce your spiritual beliefs however you see fit. There's room for them in this system, and there is much to be learned about yourself through the lens of your beliefs. This is why the two have become a popular pairing and definitely aid each other. If it helps you to use things like scripture to set your goals or provide you with more self-awareness, that's absolutely something that you can do within your own individual Enneagram journey and through the journey of your relationship.

Conclusion

The Enneagram or the Enneagram of Personality is a psychological phenomenon that very few people are aware of, and it stems from the Greek words ennea which means nine and gramma which means written. The Enneagram model that you had just read about in this eBook is what represents the psyche which is revealed by the 9 personality types that are interconnected.

Studies that were conducted at Iowa State University had shown the psychological beneficial effects on people after they had learned about themselves through the Enneagram. And it has been shown to have positive effects on young adults as well because after they learn about themselves through the Enneagram model, they have a much easier time accepting themselves. And this means that regardless of your age once you learn about who you are based on what the Enneagram model reveals, you have a chance to know yourself better and to find a way to heal as well.

It is unclear as to who had established the teachings of the Enneagram. It is believed that it is possible that either the late psychologist Oscar Ichazo or Claudio Naranjo had brought out the awareness of the Enneagram model. And the teachings by Naranjo may have been derived from the work that the late psychologist George Gurdjieff had done as well.

Either way regardless of who had been teaching others about the Enneagram model had created a great thing by creating the awareness about this amazing tool that can be quite healing. And at the end of the eBook, there will be an Enneagram test for you to take so you can discover your personality type. However, before getting to that, it is time to review the summary of the 9 personality types so you can refer back to it after taking the test instead of going back to the longer versions in the previous chapters on each of the personalities:

- **Type One - The Perfectionist** - The Ones are idealistic to the point that they need to get everything that they complete in a perfect way and expect perfection from others as well. They do possess excellent self-discipline and are quite purposeful. However, they are not realistic about the fact that everything that they or anyone else can be done perfectly. And this is what frustrates them the most because perfection can never be attained which is why they have a difficult time resting.

- **Type Two - The Helper** - The Twos are extremely caring and demonstrative, and they go out of their way to help others, hence their name. However, they do these things for a catch. The catch is that they must feel as if they are adequately appreciated. If they do not feel that they are appreciated for their good deeds, then they become possessive and irrational.

They will only back off if they feel they have been acknowledged for the good that they had done for others.

- **Type Three - The Performer** - The Threes are very success-driven, image-conscious, and ambitious, and will never settle for not achieving the best regardless of what is important to them. They are quite adaptive which is a good trait. However, they will go through great lengths to succeed even at the expense of others. They never accept failure.

- **Type Four - The Romantic** - This type is the individualist, withdrawn, and incredibly unique. They can be quite dramatic, temperamental, and are quite self-centered or absorbed. They also want to make themselves known, and they are quite creative and are quite expressive through their creativity. This type is seen as eccentric and as much as they don't like clones, they also deeply envy those who meet society's standards because of the fact that the Fours feel quite misunderstood.

- **Type Five - The Investigator** - The Fives are the types that are also withdrawn like the Fours, but they don't want to make themselves known in any way as they live as hermits while they observe and learn from what is going on around them. They make discoveries on their own as well. They are also quite innovative and will only socialize with those who are just like them, in private.

- **Type Six - The Loyalist** - The Sixes need their security, and they constantly want to trust something or someone, but they rarely put their guard down due to the fact that they are terrified of being hurt. Even if someone or something does not pose a threat to them at all, they will still find a reason not to trust, and they will always find a reason to remain suspicious. Even though the Sixes are incredibly anxious, they are also quite responsible.

- **Type Seven - The Enthusiast** - The Sevens are the type to not be able to sit still and live in the moment. They will constantly look forward to the next best thing as they are never satisfied with being done with any experience that they have. This means the Sevens will be automatically booking their next trip or adventure after finishing the one they had, and it is an ongoing situation. The Sevens are not responsible and are quite scattered. However, they are quite fun loving and are the ones that will make sure someone has a good time. This personality type is all about having fun and living the high life on a consistent basis. They will never settle for the mundane and crave for freedom.

- **Type Eight - The Challenger** - The Eights are the types who demand to be in control whether or not it is of themselves, of others, or any situation they are in. They are quite decisive and practical as well. they are quite willful, domineering, self-confident and do not hesitate to be confrontational if needed. This is the most powerful personality type on the Enneagram model.

- **Type Nine - The Peacemaker** - The Nines are self-effacing as well as having a desperate need for peace as they do what they can to avoid confrontation. They are complacent and are quite easy-going. They will be the type to put their own needs last, and they are quite agreeable and receptive. The Nines are also reassuring, and they are the ones who will provide comfort to those who are needing it.

Now that you have read the summaries of the 9 personality types, there are also the wings as well as the centers of the Enneagram model that have a large influence on the personality types which were also covered previously in the eBook.

The wings of the Enneagram are the neighboring personalities that have an influence on each personality type. The wings are there to help keep those of each personality type balanced even though they will never replace the core type. And, the centers of the Enneagram model represent the imbalances that are present in the personality types.

The centers consist of 3 different groups which were covered in the previous chapter, and each center contains 3 personality types that share the traits of the center that is affecting them.

That sums up the Enneagram model which you may want to study even in further detail. However, the one thing you will want to do in order to learn more about yourself is to take the

Enneagram test so you can discover your personality type in the final chapter which is the one following this conclusion.

The Enneagram Test Where You Can Discover Your Personality

Are you ready to discover your personality type on the Enneagram model? You now have the opportunity to do so as what you will do is answer the following questions honestly in each section which will go from A to I. Then after you are finished, you will then find out your personality type after following some basic instructions after you are completed with the test. And remember, answer these questions honestly in order to get a true answer on the personality type you really are.

All you need to do is answer the questions in each section yes or no by circling the one that applies, and once you are done, you will find out your personality type after following an easy task! Let's now begin by answering the questions in section A below.

Section A

1. Are you easily motivated to succeed no matter what it takes? Yes No

2. Are you extremely focused on your appearance? Yes No

3. Do you jump at every chance you get to become the leader? Yes No

4. After you make a mistake, do you learn from it? Yes No

5. Are you naturally competitive? Yes No

6. Do you become upset if you learn that someone else has become successful in the same niche as you? Yes No

7. Do you find intimacy difficult? Yes No

8. Has anyone ever complimented you on how charismatic and charming you are? Yes No

9. Does happiness equal success in your eyes?

Yes No

10. Do you consider yourself to be practical? Yes No

This concludes section A, now answer the questions asked in section B.

Section B

1. Does socializing make you uncomfortable? Yes No

2. Do you feel that you lack the inner strength to face life? Yes No

3. Does learning new things on a daily basis make you happy? Yes No

4. Are you naturally shy? Yes No

5. Do you feel if you ask others for help that you are imposing in any way? Yes No

6. Do you believe that intelligence is a gift and is beautiful? Yes No

7. Do you have a difficult time expressing your

emotions? Yes No

8. Do you have a strong need for privacy often? Yes No

9. Has anyone ever told you that you seem to be generally apathetic or indifferent even though it is untrue? Yes No

10. Do you consider yourself to be an expert on the things that you are strongly interested in? Yes No

That concludes section B, now answer the yes and no question in section C honestly.

Section C

1. Do you feel like you are frequently misunderstood? Yes No

2. Have you always believed you were different ever since childhood and did you consider yourself to be an outcast? Yes No

3. Are you naturally creative and intuitive? Yes No

4. Do you dislike others that try too hard to fit in?
Yes No

5. Do you feel your life is more complicated than anyone else's? Yes No

6. Do you find yourself frequently envious of others because you perceive them as having an easier life than you? Yes No

7. Are you prone to depression, or have you been officially diagnosed with any type of depressive disorder? Yes No

8. Do you daydream often to the point that you would consider yourself to be a maladaptive daydreamer? Yes No

9. Has anyone ever told you that they thought you were quite self-absorbed? Yes No

10. Do you believe that a part of you is defective? Yes No

That concludes section C, and the questions for section D will be asked below. Be sure to circle yes or no after each question.

Section D

1. Are you upset frequently that nothing you do or that others do is 'good enough'? Yes No

2. Do you strive to make order out of chaos? Yes No

3. Are you ashamed of feeling any hint of anger? Yes No

4. Do you consider yourself to be overly serious and have a hard time finding humor in anything? Yes No

5. Do you consider yourself as frequently impatient and frustrated at yourself and at others? Yes No

6. Do you think of yourself as judgmental? Yes No

7. Do you consider yourself to be a loyal friend to your friends and a loyal partner to your partner if you are in a relationship? Yes No

8. Do you feel the need to follow the rules by the book, and do you expect others to do the same? Yes No

9. Are you extremely organized? Yes   No

10. Do you think of yourself as a great leader? Yes No

That part concludes section D, and please answer the yes and no questions honestly in section E.

Section E

1. Do you fear confrontation? Yes No

2. Do you consider yourself as an optimist? Yes No

3. Do you see the good in every situation whereas others would not? Yes No

4. Do you have an easier time adapting to new situations than you initially had thought you could? Yes No

5. Do you find yourself to be slow to anger but

once you have had enough, you lose your temper? Yes No

6. Are you considerably a tolerant person? Yes No

7. Do you have an appreciation for nature to the point that you see nature as your home? Yes No

8. Do you frequently go above and beyond to help others without expecting anything in return? Yes No

9. Do you get upset when others that you care about are upset, or are you happy when others you care about are happy? Yes No

10. Do you feel you were born to be a parent or a caretaker? Yes No

That concludes section E and now answer the yes and no questions honestly in the section below, F.

Section F

1. Do you have the need to be needed by others

constantly? Yes No

2. If someone is in trouble, are you the first one that is at their rescue? Yes No

3. Do you like to invite people over to your home often? Yes No

4. Do you become very upset when you feel you have been taken for granted? Yes No

5. Have you experienced burnout on a consistent basis? Yes No

6. Has anyone ever accused you of being bossy? Yes No

7. Are you in a caregiving profession such as a nurse? Yes No

8. Do you consider yourself as possessive over your loved ones? Yes No

9. If you are a parent, are you overprotective of your child or children? Yes No

10. If you are a parent of adult children, have

they distanced themselves from you because you need to know every detail of their lives? Yes No

That concludes section F, and now we are onto section G, and please answer the yes and no questions honestly.

Section G

1. Do you always have the need to be in control whether it is controlling yourself, other people, as well as circumstances around you? Yes No

2. Are you highly ambitious? Yes   No

3. Do you usually have a very strong appetite, and do you have a tendency to overeat without feeling any pangs of guilt? Yes No

4. Have you been able to find a way to become successfully financially independent even during trying times? Yes   No

5. Do you have a hard time allowing yourself to be relaxed during intimate moments? Yes   No

6. Do you avoid feeling vulnerable for any reason

at all costs?

7. Do you feel you have uncontrollable anger issues, especially if you feel that someone or something is trying to control you or if you believe you have been betrayed? Yes   No

8. Are you overprotective of those who you care about the most? Yes   No

9. Do you make yourself appear to be tough on the outside in order to hide any sensitive or soft spots on the inside because you do not want it seen? Yes No

10. Did you bully others when you were younger who appeared to be weaker than you? Yes   No

That concludes section G, and now for the following section, H, you will need to answer the yes and no questions honestly as well.

Section H

1. Do you feel that people and anything, in general, are hard to trust? Yes   No

2. If something positive happens, do you fear that the other shoe will drop because things are just simply too good to be true? Yes   No

3. Do you believe that if a friend that you did once trust who had let you down still has good intentions? Yes   No

4. Do you keep hoping that a pleasant situation from the past will reappear? Yes   No

5. Do you have a need to stick to a routine because the idea of any kind of change frightens you? Yes   No

6. Do you prefer to work in a mundane office 9 to 5 job doing repetitive work or a job that is not overly stimulating over anything else? Yes No

7. if you are an adult, do you still live at home because the idea of moving away terrifies you? Yes No

8. Do you believe that if someone is unusually nice that they must have an ulterior motive? Yes No

9. Have you been diagnosed with any type of anxiety disorder or do you suspect you have one? Yes No

10. Did you suffer from intense separation anxiety when you were a child that took you a long time to overcome? Yes No

Now that concludes section H, and now onto the final section of this test, section I. Please answer the yes and no questions as honestly as you can.

Section I

1. Do you have a hard time staying in the moment? Yes No

2. Are you overly excited about the next possible thing that could come up? Yes No

3. Are you usually extroverted to the point that you despise being on your own? Yes No

4. Were you one of the popular kids when you were in school? Yes No

5. Are you spontaneous to the point that you

would run somewhere if you felt you needed to even before finishing a meal? Yes No

6. Do you have a difficult time sitting still or slowing down? Yes No

7. Do you have a great desire to meet a celebrity or have you gone through great lengths to meet a celebrity? Yes No

8. Do you consider yourself to be fun, and do people flock to you for that reason? Yes No

9. Do you consider yourself to be a master multi-tasker? Yes   No

10. Have you suffered from additions of any kind? Yes No

That concludes the Enneagram test where you can discover your personality.

The next thing you need to do in order to find out what your personality type is to go through each of the sections you had filled out from A to I and add up the highest amount of questions where you had answered Yes.

After doing that, you can go in the next section where the answers are and make the determination of where your personality falls on the Enneagram model.

Your Personality Type Can Be Found Right Here

Now you have the answers to the questions you had answered while you had taken the test. And if you had answered Yes to most of the questions asked in each of the sections, your personality type will be revealed which you will find below:

if you answered Yes to most of the questions in Section A, then fall into the Type 3- The Performer personality.

If you had answered Yes to most of the questions in Section B, then you are in the.

Type 5 - The Investigator group.

If you had answered Yes to most of the questions

asked in Section C, then you fall into the Type 4 - The Romantic personality group.

If you had answered Yes to most of the questions asked in Section D, then you most definitely fall into the Type 1 - The Perfectionist group.

If you had answered Yes to most of the questions in Section E, then you are in Type 9 - The Peacemaker group.

If you had answered Yes to most of the questions asked in Section F, then you are in Type 2 - The Helper group.

If you had answered Yes to most of the questions asked in Section G, then you are in Type 8 - The Challenger group.

If you said Yes to most of the questions asked in section H, then you fall into the Type 6 - The Loyalist group.

If you said Yes to most of the questions asked in section I, then you fall into the Type 7 - The Enthusiast group.

And the last question that will be asked is once you have made this discovery, does it resonate with you? And since this is quite eye-opening, what more can you learn about yourself? Finding out your Enneagram personality type will now provide you the doorway to the healing that you will benefit from if you are open to that. Either way, you now know more about yourself than you did before reading this eBook.

References

Baron, R., & Wagele, E. (1994). *Enneagram Made Easy: Discover the 9 Types of People.* HarperSanFrancisco.

Ichazo, O. (1982). *Interviews with Oscar Ichazo.* New York: Arica Institute Press.

Naranjo, C. M. (1994). *Character and neurosis - an integrative view.* Gateways Books & Tapes,us.

Riso, D. R., & Hudson, R. (1996). *Personality types: Using the Enneagram for self-discovery.* Boston: Houghton Mifflin.